5 STEPS TO A ➤ 5

500

AP Microeconomics
Questions

to know by test day

Also in the 5 Steps series:

5 Steps to a 5: AP Macroeconomics 2017
5 Steps to a 5: AP Macroeconomics 2017 Cross Platform Prep Course
5 Steps to a 5: AP Microeconomics 2017
5 Steps to a 5: AP Microeconomics 2017 Cross Platform Prep Course
5 Steps to a 5: AP Microeconomics/Macroeconomics Flashcards
5 Steps to a 5: AP Microeconomics/Macroeconomics Flashcards for Your iPod
5 Steps to a 5: AP Microeconomics/Macroeconomics (iPhone App)
5 Steps to a 5: AP Microeconomics/Macroeconomics Flashcards (iPhone App)

Also in the 500 AP Questions to Know by Test Day series:

5 Steps to a 5: 500 AP Biology Questions to Know by Test Day, Second Edition
5 Steps to a 5: 500 AP Calculus AB/BC Questions to Know by Test Day
5 Steps to a 5: 500 AP Chemistry Questions to Know by Test Day, Second Edition
5 Steps to a 5: 500 AP English Language Questions to Know by Test Day, Second Edition
5 Steps to a 5: 500 AP English Literature Questions to Know by Test Day
5 Steps to a 5: 500 AP Environmental Science Questions to Know by Test Day, Second Edition
5 Steps to a 5: 500 AP European History Questions to Know by Test Day, Second Edition
5 Steps to a 5: 500 AP Human Geography to Know by Test Day, Second Edition
5 Steps to a 5: 500 AP Macroeconomics Questions to Know by Test Day, Second Edition
5 Steps to a 5: 500 AP Physics 1 Questions to Know by Test Day, Second Edition
5 Steps to a 5: 500 AP Physics C Questions to Know by Test Day
5 Steps to a 5: 500 AP Psychology Questions to Know by Test Day, Second Edition
5 Steps to a 5: 500 AP Statistics Questions to Know by Test Day, Second Edition
5 Steps to a 5: 500 AP U.S. Government & Politics Questions to Know by Test Day
5 Steps to a 5: 500 AP U.S. History Questions to Know by Test Day, Second Edition
5 Steps to a 5: 500 AP World History Questions to Know by Test Day, Second Edition

5 STEPS TO A >5

500
AP Microeconomics
Questions
to know by test day

SECOND EDITION

Anaxos, Inc.

Brian Reddington

New York   Chicago   San Francisco   Athens   London   Madrid
Mexico City   Milan   New Delhi   Singapore   Sydney   Toronto

Anaxos, Inc. (Austin, TX) has been creating education and reference materials for over fifteen years. Based in Austin, Texas, the company uses writers from across the globe who offer expertise on an array of subjects just as expansive.

Brian Reddington earned his bachelor's degree in history from Stony Brook University in Stony Brook, New York, before pursuing a master's degree in special education at Queens College in New York City. A dedicated educator, he has been teaching economics since 2008. He lives in Bellmore, New York, with his wife and two young daughters, Anna June and Sarah Gretchen.

1 2 3 4 5 6 7 8 9   QFR   21 20 19 18 17 16

ISBN   978-1-259-83661-9
MHID   1-259-83661-4

e-ISBN   978-1-259-83662-6
e-MHID   1-259-83662-2

McGraw-Hill Education products are available at special quantity discounts to use as premiums and sales promotions or for use in corporate training programs. To contact a representative, please visit the Contact Us pages at www.mhprofessional.com.

CONTENTS

INTRODUCTION

Congratulations! You've taken a big step toward AP success by purchasing *5 Steps to a 5: 500 AP Microeconomics Questions to Know by Test Day*. We are here to help you take the next step and score high on your AP exam so you can earn college credits and get into the college or university of your choice. This book gives you 500 AP-style multiple-choice questions that cover all the most essential course material. Each question has a detailed answer explanation. These questions will give you valuable independent practice to supplement your regular textbook and the groundwork you are already doing in your AP classroom. This and the other books in this series were written by expert AP teachers who know your exam inside out and can identify the crucial exam information as well as questions that are most likely to appear on the exam.

You might be the kind of student who takes several AP courses and needs to study extra questions a few weeks before the exam for a final review. Or you might be the kind of student who puts off preparing until the last weeks before the exam. No matter what your preparation style is, you will surely benefit from reviewing these 500 questions, which closely parallel the content, format, and degree of difficulty of the questions on the actual AP exam. These questions and their answer explanations are the ideal last-minute study tool for those final few weeks before the test.

Remember the old saying "Practice makes perfect." If you practice with all the questions and answers in this book, we are certain you will build the skills and confidence you need to do great on the exam. Good luck!

—Editors of McGraw-Hill Education

CHAPTER 1

Basic Economic Concepts

1. The study of economics is correctly defined as
   (A) the methods used to supply our limited material wants with unlimited physical resources
   (B) how best to predict the fluctuations in the stock market
   (C) how best to supply our unlimited wants with limited and scarce material resources
   (D) the methods used to disseminate limited resources among a population's scarce material wants
   (E) the study of the interaction and allocation of limited resources and market structures

2. Deirdre has one free hour to practice the piano for an upcoming school concert or work at the library for $7 per hour or babysit her neighbor's 12-year-old son for $10 per hour. She chooses to practice the piano. What is the opportunity cost of practicing the piano?
   (A) The opportunity cost would be $17 because she chose not to participate in these activities.
   (B) Without knowing the marginal value of practicing the piano, there is no way of knowing the true opportunity cost.
   (C) The opportunity cost would be $20 because she needs to babysit for two hours to earn a profit.
   (D) The opportunity cost would be $10 because it is the wage for the most profitable alternative.
   (E) The opportunity cost would be $3 because it is the monetary difference between two alternative choices.

3. After dedicating two hours to studying for the AP economics exam, Seth chooses to spend an additional hour studying. Which of the following is most likely TRUE?

    (A) The marginal benefit of the additional hour is at least as great as the marginal cost of the additional hour.

    (B) The marginal cost of the additional hour is less than the marginal benefit of the additional hour.

    (C) Both the marginal benefit and marginal cost are always equal in this scenario.

    (D) The marginal benefit of the second hour is less than the marginal benefit of the additional hour.

    (E) The marginal cost of the second hour is greater than the marginal cost of the additional hour.

4. Which of these choices is NOT a factor of production?

    (A) capital, the machinery, factories, and industrial equipment used to produce goods

    (B) labor, the human work hours used during production

    (C) entrepreneurship, input by the decision maker who allocates production factors

    (D) land, including natural resources such as oil and timber reserves as well as land itself

    (E) money, the financial capital used to purchase goods and services used in production

5. The concave shape of the production possibilities curve implies the notion of

    (A) increasing opportunity costs

    (B) comparative advantage

    (C) marginal analysis

    (D) allocation of limited resources with unlimited material wants

    (E) MB = MC

6. It is beneficial for two countries to trade only when there is

    (A) a mutually beneficial trade agreement

    (B) increasing returns to scale

    (C) decreasing returns to scale

    (D) an absolute advantage in production between the two countries

    (E) a comparative advantage in production between the two countries

7. If a society overallocates its resources, then
   - (A) consumer spending would increase due to an increase in demand
   - (B) marginal benefit would be greater than marginal cost
   - (C) the opportunity cost of producing one more unit would increase exponentially
   - (D) marginal benefit would be less than marginal cost
   - (E) marginal benefit would equal marginal cost

8. Richard and Michele have to mow their lawn and walk their dog on Sunday morning. It takes Richard one hour to either mow the lawn or walk the dog. Michele can also walk the dog in one hour, but she needs two hours to mow the lawn. What should Richard and Michele do?
   - (A) Michele should walk the dog because she has absolute advantage in mowing the lawn.
   - (B) Richard should walk the dog because he has comparative advantage in mowing the lawn.
   - (C) Richard should mow the lawn because he has comparative advantage in mowing the lawn.
   - (D) Michele should mow the lawn because she has comparative advantage in mowing the lawn.
   - (E) Richard should walk the dog because he has comparative advantage in walking the dog.

9. In a command economy,
   - (A) market prices are determined through supply and demand
   - (B) market prices are determined through supply and demand and some government interventions
   - (C) market prices are determined by a central plan designed by the government
   - (D) market prices are determined through supply and demand and some barter system
   - (E) market prices are determined through the resources backing of the gold and silver supply

10. Which of the following will cause an outward shift of the production possibilities curve?

    (A) educational training for employees

    (B) a decrease in a nation's birthrate, thus decreasing the labor force

    (C) a natural disaster creating extreme limitations of a vital natural resource

    (D) a shortage of skilled workers

    (E) an increase of unskilled workers

11. A point lying directly on the production possibilities curve is

    (A) productively efficient

    (B) unattainable, yet productively efficient

    (C) attainable and productively efficient

    (D) unattainable

    (E) productively inefficient

12. *Scarcity* is best defined as

    (A) material resources are unlimited

    (B) an idea used by industrializing nations to satisfy unlimited wants and desires with limited natural resources

    (C) limited vital material resources compared with limited wants and needs

    (D) all points lying inside the production possibilities curve

    (E) the idea that a society's wants and needs are unlimited, and material resources are limited

13. Joe works as a manager at a fast-food restaurant. He has enough supplies to make 500 hot dogs and 400 hamburgers to sell to customers. If he uses all of his supplies to make hot dogs, he could make 1,000 hot dogs and no hamburgers. If he uses all of his supplies to make hamburgers instead, he could make 800 hamburgers and no hot dogs. What is Joe's opportunity cost if he uses all of his supplies to make hot dogs?

    (A) The opportunity cost is 800 hamburgers because this is the maximum quantity of hamburgers that Joe could make.
    (B) The opportunity cost is 400 hamburgers because this is what Joe is giving up to make hot dogs.
    (C) The opportunity cost is 500 hot dogs because this is the increase in hot dog production.
    (D) The opportunity cost is 1,000 hot dogs because this is the amount of hot dogs produced.
    (E) The prices of hot dogs and hamburgers are necessary to calculate opportunity cost in this example.

14. Mineral deposits, human capital, entrepreneurship, and use of technology and machinery are all examples of
    (A) factors of production
    (B) superior and inferior goods
    (C) elements sometimes needed to move an existing company overseas
    (D) public goods
    (E) material wants and needs

15. The law of increasing costs is best defined as
    (A) when the price of a good rises, the quantity does not fall
    (B) more of a product is produced, the greater its opportunity cost
    (C) one obtains more of a good, the marginal utility (the value from one more unit) will decrease
    (D) the economy grows, government spending will increase as well
    (E) all costs are opportunity costs

16. The production possibilities curve will show a straight line if which of the following is TRUE?

   (A) Resources are equally suitable for the production of both goods.
   (B) Vital resources for the good are limitless.
   (C) The economy is performing below maximum efficiency and output.
   (D) The law of decreasing marginal utility does not apply.
   (E) Marginal benefit is less than marginal cost.

17. A country is said to have a comparative advantage over another country when

   (A) it can produce a good at a lower opportunity cost than another country
   (B) it can produce a good using more resources per unit of output than another country
   (C) there is a higher degree of specialization and division of labor compared to another country
   (D) when comparing each country's production possibilities frontiers, one country is operating at maximum efficiency and output
   (E) one country's production possibilities frontier is shifted farther to the right compared to another country's production possibilities frontier

18. How is it possible for a country to consume more than its production possibilities curve dictates?

   (A) not possible without greater quantities of the factors of production already obtained
   (B) specialization
   (C) increase in education and job training
   (D) obtainment of a greater quantity of affordable substitutes
   (E) increase in the division of labor

19. Suppose both Spain and Germany produce soccer balls and golf balls. Spain can produce soccer balls at a lower opportunity cost than Germany. Germany can produce golf balls at a lower opportunity cost than Spain. According to the law of comparative advantage,

    (A) Germany should stop producing soccer balls; Spain should stop producing golf balls; Spain and Germany should establish a trade for the product they stopped producing.
    (B) Germany should stop producing golf balls; Spain should stop producing soccer balls.
    (C) Germany should increase production of golf balls and decrease the production of soccer balls.
    (D) Spain should increase the production of soccer balls and decrease the production of golf balls.
    (E) none of the above

20. Which of the following are some of the basic questions every economy must answer?
    (A) What to produce? How to produce? For whom to produce?
    (B) When to produce? How to produce? How much to produce?
    (C) For whom to produce? When to produce? What to produce?
    (D) What to produce? How to produce? Where to produce?
    (E) all of the above

21. Economic growth is only possible if
    (A) all of the fundamental questions an economy faces are answered
    (C) there is a decrease in resources and decreasing opportunity costs
    (B) there is a highly developed division of labor
    (D) there is an increase in resources and technological advancements in production
    (E) there is a diseconomy of scale

22. As a rule, one should purchase a good or engage in an activity if
    (A) the opportunity cost is more than the value of the good or activity
    (B) the marginal benefit is greater or equal to the marginal cost
    (C) there is a decreasing marginal value of return
    (D) there is an increasing marginal value of return
    (E) the marginal benefit is less than or equal to the marginal cost

23. Your school decides to build a new performing arts center. What is the opportunity cost of the performing arts center?
    (A) the money used in construction of the performing arts center
    (B) the cost of building the performing arts center now rather than waiting until next year
    (C) any other good or service that cannot be provided right now due to resources used for the new performing arts center
    (D) cannot be determined without knowing what the next best option was for using the resources that went to the performing arts center
    (E) none of the above

24. All are reasons why a production possibilities curve will shift to the right EXCEPT
    (A) the quantity of resources increases
    (B) the quality of existing resources increases
    (C) technological advancements in production
    (D) the labor force increases
    (E) the economy is operating at allocative efficiency

25. *Marginal analysis* is best defined as
    (A) the additional benefit received from the consumption of the next unit of a good or service
    (B) the additional cost from the consumption of the next unit of a good or service
    (C) analyzing the combination of goods and services that provide the best benefit to society
    (D) making decisions based upon the marginal benefits and marginal costs of that decision
    (E) when businesses use their resources to produce goods and services for which they have a comparative advantage

26. An economic system is characterized as emphasizing private property and competition, and prices inform buyers and sellers how to allocate their resources. No public sector exists in the country. This economic system would be known as a

    (A) mixed system
    (B) market system
    (C) socialist system
    (D) command system
    (E) barter system

27. Economic systems differ most in

    (A) increasing returns to scale
    (B) the quality of goods and services produced
    (C) how they answer the fundamental economic questions all societies must answer
    (D) production possibility frontiers
    (E) the quantity of goods and services produced

28. As a result of the scarcity of resources,

    (A) every society must commit to central planning
    (B) the government must decide how best to use those resources
    (C) there is the unavoidable reality of poverty
    (D) every society must choose how best to use those resources
    (E) every society must include elements of a market economy and government planning

29. When production takes place at a point on the production possibilities curve, and MB = MC, production is

    (A) productively efficient but not allocatively efficient
    (B) allocatively efficient but not productively efficient
    (C) productively efficient and allocatively efficient
    (D) neither productively efficient nor allocatively efficient
    (E) none of the above

30. The basic economic questions being answered by the decisions of buyers and sellers in the marketplace occur in a
    (A) mixed economy
    (B) command economy
    (C) traditional economy
    (D) market economy
    (E) barter economy

Refer to the following graph for questions 31 and 32.

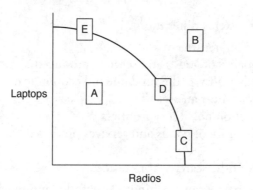

31. A production possibilities curve passing through which point on the graph would indicate a recession?
    (A) point A
    (B) point B
    (C) point C
    (D) point D
    (E) point E

32. What would a shift in production from point E on the graph to point D indicate?
    (A) Laptop production declined, indicating a possible recession.
    (B) Radio production increased, indicating an expanding economy.
    (C) The firm became more efficient at radio production and less efficient at laptop production.
    (D) The firm decided to produce more radios and fewer laptops and its current production capacity hasn't changed.
    (E) Laptop supply costs are rising.

33. What would cause the production possibilities curve to shift to the left?

(A) an increase in the availability of raw materials
(B) factory capacity expansion
(C) a decision to produce more of one item and less of another
(D) shorter work hours
(E) less vacation time

34. Using the Law of Variable Proportions, when should a restaurant stop hiring new workers?

(A) when production per worker stops increasing
(B) when each additional worker results in less production
(C) when the additional output for the next worker equals the cost of employing the next worker
(D) when unmet demand no longer exists for the restaurant's food
(E) only when the restaurant purchases new kitchen equipment

35. A country allows buyers and sellers to make their own choices. Ownership of private property is allowed, but the government owns companies in key industries and makes production decisions for these industries. What type of economy does this country have?

(A) a command economy
(B) a traditional economy
(C) a mixed economy
(D) a market economy
(E) a barter economy

36. What is an example of the paradox of value?

(A) gasoline costing more per gallon than crude oil
(B) solar power costing more per watt than coal power
(C) acid rain caused by power plant emissions
(D) rubies costing more than bottled water
(E) a steak costing more than a hamburger

37. What item is considered a durable good?

(A) a box of pasta
(B) a truck
(C) a T-shirt
(D) a pair of shoes
(E) a cartridge of printer ink

38. Buyers and sellers exchange goods and services directly without trading them for money in which type of economy?

(A) a mixed economy
(B) a market economy
(C) a barter economy
(D) a command economy
(E) a traditional economy

39. A tire factory is hiring employees at a wage of $30,000 per year. Adding the first employee allows the company to produce tires worth $50,000 each year. The tenth employee would increase tire production by $30,000 per year. The eleventh employee would increase tire production by $25,000 per year. Hiring a twentieth employee would not increase tire production at all. How many employees should the company hire?

(A) The tire factory should hire one employee because MB > MC.
(B) The tire factory should hire 10 employees because MB = MC.
(C) The tire factory should hire 11 employees because MB < MC.
(D) The tire factory should hire 20 employees because it breaks even at this point.
(E) The tire factory should hire more than 20 workers.

40. Which situation best illustrates the concept of marginal utility?

(A) A nation trades goods for which it has a comparative advantage.
(B) A state raises taxes on jewelry.
(C) A consumer purchases three cans of soda but does not want to buy a fourth can.
(D) Gold increases in value compared with the euro.
(E) Taxes increase to fund health care and retirement benefits.

41. France and Switzerland produce cheese and chocolate. France has a competitive advantage in cheese production while Switzerland has a competitive advantage in chocolate production. If France places a trade embargo on Switzerland, what is likely to happen with cheese and chocolate production in each country?

(A) France will produce more cheese and Switzerland will produce more chocolate.

(B) France will produce more chocolate and Switzerland will produce more cheese.

(C) France will produce less chocolate and Switzerland will produce less cheese.

(D) France will produce less chocolate and Switzerland will produce more cheese.

(E) France will produce more cheese and Switzerland will produce less chocolate.

The following graph shows a nation's production possibilities curve. Use this graph for questions 42 and 43.

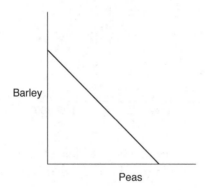

42. What does this curve indicate about the nation producing these two crops?

(A) The curve is not valid because a production possibilities curve must be concave.

(B) The nation's resources are equally suitable for barley or pea production.

(C) With each additional unit of barley not produced, the nation can produce a larger amount of peas.

(D) With each additional unit of peas not produced, the nation can produce a larger amount of barley.

(E) The nation has increasing opportunity costs.

43. What would happen if the nation developed specialized resources for barley and pea production?

    (A) The curve would become concave but would not shift left or right.

    (B) The curve would shift to the left and remain flat.

    (C) The curve would shift to the right and remain flat.

    (D) The curve would become convex.

    (E) The curve would shift to the right and become concave.

The following graph shows the production possibilities curve for a bakery that produces cookies and loaves of bread. Refer to this graph for questions 44 and 45.

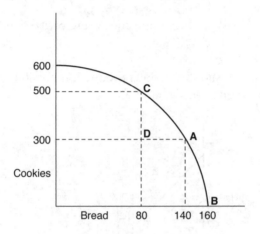

44. The bakery is currently producing 140 loaves of bread. If it decides to produce 160 loaves of bread instead, what is the opportunity cost for the bakery?

    (A) 200 cookies

    (B) 600 cookies

    (C) 500 cookies

    (D) 300 cookies

    (E) 100 cookies

45. If the bakery is producing cookies and bread at point A on the production possibilities curve, and then one of its ovens breaks down and its production moves to point D, what is the opportunity cost of the broken oven?

(A) 80 units of bread
(B) 140 units of bread
(C) 60 units of bread
(D) 200 cookies
(E) 300 cookies

This production possibilities curve shows bread and car production possibilities for a nation. Refer to it for questions 46 and 47.

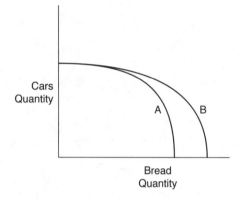

46. If the nation's production shifts from point A to point B, this represents

(A) an economic expansion
(B) a recession
(C) the introduction of a biased technology for car manufacturing
(D) the introduction of a biased technology for bread manufacturing
(E) a decline in bread production efficiency

47. A shift in production from point A to point B results in

(A) a higher bread quantity
(B) a lower car quantity
(C) a higher car quantity
(D) the same car quantity
(E) both A and D

48. A nation produces spinach and lettuce. A biased technology is introduced that improves spinach production. If the quantity of spinach produced does not change, the

(A) lettuce quantity will increase
(B) lettuce quantity will stay the same
(C) lettuce quantity will fall
(D) production possibilities curve will shift to the left
(E) maximum production quantity for lettuce will increase

The following graph shows production possibility curves for Britain and France. Refer to it for questions 49 and 50.

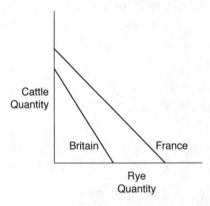

49. In terms of comparative advantage,

(A) Britain has a comparative advantage for cattle
(B) Britain has a comparative advantage for rye
(C) France has a comparative advantage for cattle
(D) France has a comparative advantage for rye
(E) A and D.

50. Production is allocatively efficient at a point

(A) anywhere on the production possibilities curve
(B) where marginal benefit equals marginal cost
(C) to the right of the production possibilities curve
(D) to the left of the production possibilities curve
(E) where marginal benefit exceeds marginal cost

The Nature and Function of Product Markets

51. What will most likely result if the price of apples decreases?

(A) The quantity of apples demanded will increase.
(B) The supply of apples will decrease.
(C) The demand for apples will increase.
(D) The quantity of apples supplied will decrease.
(E) none of the above

52. If Michael's average yearly income increases, and it is observed that his demand for steak has increased, then steak must be considered

(A) an inferior good
(B) a normal good
(C) a determinant of demand
(D) a determinant of supply
(E) a necessity

53. If Peter's average yearly income increases, and it is observed that his demand for thrift-store-bought shoes decreases, then thrift-store-bought shoes must be considered

(A) a normal good
(B) a shortage good
(C) a necessity
(D) an inferior good
(E) a determinant of demand

54. Suppose it is necessary for tin to be used in the production of guitar strings. If the price of tin decreases and all other variables are constant, what will most likely result?

(A) The demand for silver will increase.

(B) The quantity demanded for guitars will decrease.

(C) The demand for guitars will increase.

(D) The supply of guitars will decrease.

(E) The supply of guitar strings will increase.

55. According to the law of demand,

(A) as the price of a good or service increases, the demand will shift to the right

(B) as the price of a good or service increases, the demand will shift to the left

(C) there is an inverse relationship between quantity demanded of a good or service and the price of that good or service

(D) as prices for a good or service increase, consumers will begin to use substitute goods

(E) as the price of a good or service increases, the quantity demanded will increase

56. According to the law of supply,

(A) as the price of a good or service decreases, the supply will decrease

(B) as the price of a good or service increases, the quantity supplied will increase

(C) as the price of a good or service increases, the quantity demanded will increase

(D) as the price of a good or service increases, the quantity demanded will decrease

(E) there is an inverse relationship between the price of a good or service and the quantity supplied

57. Within the market system, prices are determined by

(A) supply and demand

(B) the determinants of supply and demand

(C) opportunity cost

(D) total market demand

(E) production costs

58. A hurricane destroys a significant supply of bananas in 2011. As a result, the price of bananas increases. What prediction may be made regarding the supply of apples, a substitute good, when its market is in equilibrium?

(A) The apple price rises, and the apple supply will increase.

(B) The apple quantity supplied will increase.

(C) The apple price falls, and the apple supply will decrease.

(D) The apple price falls, and the apple quantity supplied will decrease.

(E) Both the apple price and the apple quantity supplied are undetermined.

59. What is likely to happen if the price of figs increases?

(A) The supply of figs will increase.

(B) The quantity of figs demanded will decrease.

(C) The demand for figs will increase.

(D) The quantity of figs supplied will increase.

(E) none of the above

60. If the demand for tennis rackets increases, what prediction can be made regarding tennis balls?

(A) The demand for tennis balls will fall.

(B) The supply of tennis balls will remain the same.

(C) The price of tennis balls will remain the same.

(D) The supply of tennis balls will fall.

(E) The price and the quantity supplied of tennis balls will increase.

61. Which of the following situations will cause the demand curve for chicken, a normal good, to shift to the left?

(A) Consumer incomes decrease.

(B) Consumer incomes increase.

(C) The price of steak decreases.

(D) There is a decrease in the cost of raising chickens on a farm.

(E) There is a scientific discovery that relates eating chicken to lower blood pressure.

62. Bob used to eat a can of beans for dinner when he was unemployed. After he got a new job, his income increased and he started eating a hamburger for dinner instead. What types of goods are the can of beans and hamburger?
    (A) public goods
    (B) capital goods
    (C) inferior and superior goods
    (D) durable and nondurable goods
    (E) luxury and common goods

63. Mr. Harrington produces hot dog buns. Hot dogs and hot dog buns are complementary goods. He is most likely to sell his hot dog buns at a higher price if
    (A) the price of hot dogs decreases
    (B) there is an increase in consumer income
    (C) the price of hot dogs increases
    (D) a new technology is developed enabling an increase in hot dog production
    (E) a new technology is developed enabling an increase in hot dog bun production

64. The equilibrium price is established
    (A) at the next price above where the demand and supply curves intersect
    (B) when the quantity supplied equals the quantity demanded
    (C) at the next price below where the demand and supply curves intersect
    (D) when you take the difference between the two lowest points plotted on the demand and supply curves
    (E) at the price where either the demand or supply curve becomes horizontal

Refer to the following demand curve for baseballs to answer question 65.

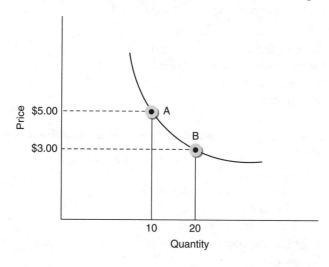

65. If the quantity demanded for baseballs shifts from point B to point A, this represents
    (A) an increase in the price of the good
    (B) an increase in consumer income
    (C) an increase in the price of a complementary good
    (D) an increase in the price of a substitute good
    (E) none of the above

66. Doherty Industries is a leading producer of an energy drink. Which of the following will cause Doherty Industries to offer more of the product at all possible sale prices?
    (A) A competitor lowers the price of the product.
    (B) The price of a key ingredient increases.
    (C) The price of a key ingredient decreases.
    (D) The demand for the energy drink decreases.
    (E) The demand is perfectly elastic.

67. Suppose the demand for a product is inelastic. If a producer wishes to increase total revenue, he or she should
    (A) decrease prices
    (B) decrease the quantity supplied
    (C) increase the quantity supplied
    (D) hire more workers
    (E) raise prices

68. Which is an important factor to make the demand for a good inelastic?
    (A) It is a necessity.
    (B) There are many substitutes.
    (C) It is a luxury item.
    (D) There are many cross-price substitutes.
    (E) A significant portion of consumers' budgets goes to purchasing the good.

69. There is a 10 percent rise in the price of bottled water. This creates a 40 percent change in the quantity demanded. The demand for bottled water is considered to be
    (A) perfectly inelastic
    (B) elastic
    (C) inelastic
    (D) perfectly elastic
    (E) none of the above

70. If a 30 percent rise in gas prices creates a 0 percent decrease in the quantity demanded, the demand is said to be
    (A) inelastic
    (B) perfectly elastic
    (C) elastic
    (D) perfectly inelastic
    (E) none of the above

71. Sally works at a clothing store and the manager has cut her weekly shift from 30 to 20 hours, reducing her income. As a result, her demand for fresh vegetables decreases and her demand for canned vegetables increases. In this example, what type of good is a can of vegetables?

(A) a shortage good
(B) an inferior good
(C) a necessity
(D) a capital good
(E) a normal good

Use the following graph to answer questions 72 and 73.

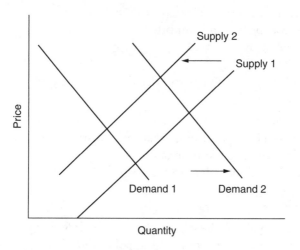

72. All of the following are factors that contributed to Demand 1 shifting to Demand 2 EXCEPT

(A) an increase in consumer income
(B) a decrease in the price of a substitute good
(C) an increase in the number of buyers in a market
(D) consumers expect the price of the good to increase in the future
(E) the product's popularity with consumers increased

73. All of the following are factors that contributed to Supply 1 shifting to Supply 2 EXCEPT

    (A) the price of a key ingredient to the product decreased
    (B) the number of sellers decreased
    (C) sellers expect the price of the good to rise in the future
    (D) the government increased a tax on the product
    (E) the product is no longer subsidized by the government

74. An effective price ceiling is usually set

    (A) above the equilibrium price and quantity
    (B) at the intersection of the supply and demand curves
    (C) by subtracting the highest price for supply and the lowest point for demand on their respective curves
    (D) below the equilibrium price
    (E) none of the above

75. Which factor contributes to price elasticity of supply?

    (A) time
    (B) consumer surplus
    (C) consumer expectations regarding future prices
    (D) producer tastes and preferences
    (E) the availability of a producer surplus

76. Consumer surplus is measured by

    (A) the area above the supply curve but below the price equilibrium
    (B) the sum of buyer and seller surplus
    (C) the area above the supply curve and above the price equilibrium
    (D) the quotient of percentage change in quantity supplied and percentage change in price
    (E) the quotient of percentage change in quantity demanded and percentage change in price

77. A grape farm uses fertilizer to produce grapes. What will occur if the price of fertilizer increases?

    (A) The demand for grapes will increase.
    (B) The quantity of grapes demanded will increase.
    (C) The supply of grapes will decrease.
    (D) The quantity of fertilizer demanded will increase.
    (E) The supply of grapes will increase.

78. If the supply curve is a line with an upward slope, an increase in demand will cause

(A) an increase in prices and a larger quantity sold
(B) an increase in prices and a smaller quantity sold
(C) a decrease in prices and a larger quantity sold
(D) a decrease in prices and a smaller quantity sold
(E) none of the above

79. A price increase in product X resulted in an increase in demand for product Z. Product Z is most likely a(n)

(A) inferior good
(B) complementary good
(C) substitute good
(D) normal good
(E) factor of production

80. A limit on interest rates charged by a credit card company is an example of a

(A) price floor
(B) price ceiling
(C) price support
(D) consequence of minimum wage law
(E) negative externality

81. When quantity demanded is greater than quantity supplied, there is a(n)

(A) negative externality
(B) shortage in the market
(C) surplus in the market
(D) increase in government regulation
(E) decrease in unemployment

82. If the price of a good increases, the most likely result would be for the

(A) quantity supplied to increase
(B) quantity supplied to decrease
(C) demand to increase
(D) supply to decrease
(E) demand to decrease

83. The notion that the actions of producers in their own self-interest will result to further the public interest is known as

    (A) the invisible hand
    (B) consumer sovereignty
    (C) the law of demand
    (D) derived demand
    (E) none of the above

84. Price, technology, taxes, and the number of producers in an industry are known as

    (A) factors of production
    (B) capital and human capital
    (C) producer expectations
    (D) determinants of supply
    (E) determinants of demand

85. Another name for *excess supply* is

    (A) disequilibrium
    (B) equilibrium point
    (C) Gini ratio
    (D) surplus
    (E) shortage

86. If a market surplus exists, establishing an effective price floor would

    (A) reduce a market surplus
    (B) increase a market surplus
    (C) remove the need for government regulation
    (D) decrease demand
    (E) increase government regulation

Use the following graph to answer question 87.

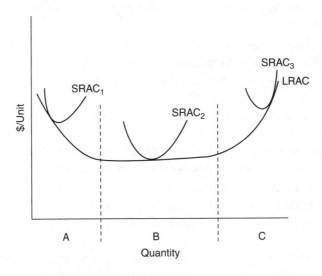

87. Sections A, B, and C of the short-run and long-run average cost graph show, respectively,

   (A) economies of scale, constant returns to scale, and diseconomies of scale
   (B) economies of scale, diseconomies of scale, and constant returns to scale
   (C) diseconomies of scale, constant returns to scale, and economies of scale
   (D) diseconomies of scale, economies of scale, and constant returns to scale
   (E) constant returns to scale, economies of scale, and diseconomies of scale

88. The number of substitutes for a good and time are known as

   (A) determinants of supply
   (B) determinants of demand
   (C) determinants of elasticity
   (D) factors of production
   (E) elements of the Gini ratio

89. A warm winter results in a larger supply of wheat for the year. Corn is a substitute good for wheat. What happens to wheat and corn prices?

    (A) The corn price stays the same and the wheat price falls.
    (B) The corn price falls and the wheat price falls.
    (C) The corn price rises and the wheat price falls.
    (D) The corn price stays the same and the wheat price rises.
    (E) The corn price and the wheat price both increase.

90. Suppose the price of iPhones increases 2 percent and the quantity demanded for iPhones decreases by 4 percent, then

    (A) elasticity is 2 and demand is price elastic
    (B) elasticity is 0.5 and demand is price inelastic
    (C) elasticity is 8 and demand is price elastic
    (D) elasticity is .05 and demand is price inelastic
    (E) answer cannot be determined without knowing the length of time the product is on the market with the increase in price

91. Demand for hamburgers increases. Hamburgers and hamburger buns are complementary goods. What happens to the demand curve for hamburger buns and the price?

    (A) The price of hamburger buns does not change and the demand curve shifts to the left.
    (B) The price of hamburger buns does not change and the demand curve shifts to the right.
    (C) The price of hamburger buns increases and the demand curve remains the same.
    (D) The price of hamburger buns increases and the demand curve shifts to the right.
    (E) The price of hamburger buns increases and the demand curve shifts to the left.

92. Suppose the market is in equilibrium for razor blades where the marginal benefit equals the marginal cost. If the government imposes a tax on razor blades, what may result?

    (A) dead weight loss
    (B) an increase in demand
    (C) an increase in supply
    (D) a price ceiling
    (E) a price floor

93. Dead weight loss refers to

(A) the lost benefit to society caused by the movement away from the market equilibrium quantity

(B) the gained benefit to suppliers caused by the increase in the market equilibrium quantity

(C) the incremental benefit or loss when the consumer increases consumption by one additional unit (marginal utility)

(D) the legal maximum price above which a product cannot be sold (price ceiling)

(E) the legal minimum price below which a product cannot be sold (price floor)

94. The law of diminishing marginal utility refers to

(A) the marginal utility from consuming one additional item will fall

(B) the marginal utility from consuming one additional item will increase

(C) marginal benefit should equal marginal cost in a market

(D) MC > MB when the market is in disequilibrium

(E) price floors help establish MB > MC

95. If you calculate the price elasticity of a good to be 0, you are correct to assume

(A) it is a normal good

(B) it is a luxury good

(C) people will buy the good regardless of the price

(D) the good has few substitutes

(E) the good has few complements

96. If there is joint demand for olives and mushrooms, then olives and mushrooms are

(A) substitute goods

(B) complementary goods

(C) normal goods

(D) inferior goods

(E) luxury goods

The following graph shows supply and demand for artichokes. Refer to it for questions 97 and 98.

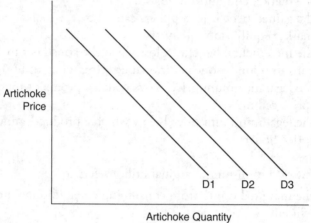

97. Bell peppers are a substitute for artichokes. If the price of bell peppers increases, demand for artichokes could shift from
    (A) D1 to D2
    (B) D2 to D1
    (C) D3 to D2
    (D) D3 to D1
    (E) demand would not change

98. Bell peppers are a substitute for artichokes. Tomatoes are also a substitute for artichokes. If a 10 percent price drop for bell peppers would shift artichoke demand from D2 to D1, and a 10 percent price drop for tomatoes would shift artichoke demand from D3 to D1, then
    (A) tomatoes are a perfect substitute
    (B) bell peppers are a perfect substitute
    (C) tomatoes are a better substitute
    (D) bell peppers are a better substitute
    (E) tomatoes and bell peppers are equally substitutable

99. If a business owns plants at various stages of production, this is known as

(A) a vertically integrated firm
(B) a multiplant firm
(C) a conglomerate
(D) a sole proprietorship
(E) an oligopoly

100. A government policy to tax producers is the possible result of

(A) spillover costs
(B) positive externalities
(C) principal-agent problem
(D) free-rider problem
(E) all of the above

101. Product differentiation is an essential part of which type of market structure?

(A) oligopoly
(B) monopoly
(C) monopolistic competition
(D) natural monopoly
(E) perfect competition

102. One of the key differences the makers of iPhone and BlackBerry smartphones utilize as part of a monopolistic competition is

(A) product differentiation
(B) patents
(C) limited liability
(D) licenses
(E) game theory

103. A business organization that pays a licensing fee to another firm for rights to produce branded goods or services is known as a(n)

(A) industry
(B) franchise
(C) partnership
(D) oligopoly
(E) firm

104. If marginal cost falls in the beginning and then gradually rises as output increases, you would know that

(A) the law of diminishing returns is valid

(B) MC = MB

(C) this market structure is a perfect competition

(D) this market structure is a monopolistic competition

(E) you would have constant returns to scale

105. All of the following are variable production inputs EXCEPT

(A) the amount of electricity used in a plant

(B) the total amount of raw materials utilized in a plant

(C) human capital

(D) the size of a firm's labor force

(E) the water bill for a plant

106. If the price of a variable resource increases, the result would be

(A) a downward shift of MC

(B) an upward shift in AFC

(C) an upward shift in MC

(D) a downward shift in ATC

(E) an upward shift in MP

107. A firm with a natural monopoly may be required by law to set prices either on or relatively close to the costs that the firm incurred to make the good or service. This idea is known as

(A) the average cost pricing rule

(B) the ability to pay rule

(C) an antitrust law

(D) law of diminishing marginal returns

(E) economies of scale

108. A monopolistic competition refers to

(A) extensive economies of scale and higher cost-efficiency when there is only one firm for the entire demand of a product

(B) many small firms offering a differentiated product with easy entry into the market

(C) a market structure with a small number of interdependent large firms producing a standardized product

(D) the most competitive market structure

(E) the least competitive market structure

109. The difference between total revenue and total explicit and implicit costs is known as

(A) economic profit
(B) accounting profit
(C) total fixed costs
(D) total variable costs
(E) total costs

110. As a result of increased growth, a firm may experience difficulty in managing larger plants and may lose efficiency. This is known as

(A) constant returns to scale
(B) explicit costs
(C) law of diminishing marginal returns
(D) diseconomies of scale
(E) economies of scale

111. If the long-run average cost curve is constant over a variety of plant sizes, this is known as

(A) diseconomies of scale
(B) economies of scale
(C) explicit costs
(D) law of diminishing marginal returns
(E) constant returns to scale

112. Specialization and lower costs of inputs will often result in

(A) a decrease in economic profits
(B) economies of scale
(C) a decrease in implicit costs
(D) constant returns to scale
(E) diseconomies of scale

113. An oligopoly refers to

(A) a single firm offering the product and achieving economies of scale
(B) the market structure where a firm has the most pricing power
(C) a small number of interdependent firms, high barriers to entry, and significant pricing power
(D) many small firms offering a differentiated product with easy entry into the market
(E) the market structure where a firm has the least pricing power

Use the following graph to answer question 114.

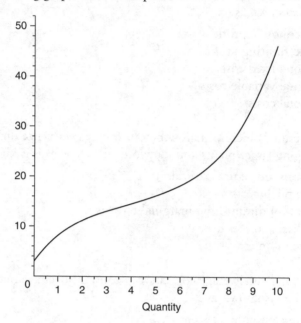

Quantity

114. The preceding graph shows
    (A) a total cost curve
    (B) a total revenue curve
    (C) no increasing returns in the early stage of production
    (D) a fixed variable cost curve
    (E) no diminishing returns

115. Mr. Ray is a business owner of a competitive firm. He is trying to decide whether to shut down his firm in the short run. Which factors should Mr. Ray analyze to help in his decision?
    (A) average variable cost and marginal revenue
    (B) total revenue and total cost
    (C) total fixed cost and total revenue
    (D) price and average total cost
    (E) price and marginal benefit

116. All of the following are part of a monopolistic competition market structure EXCEPT

(A) differentiated products
(B) dead weight loss
(C) economic profits in the short run
(D) economic profits in the long run
(E) many firms

117. In a perfect competition, if P > ATC, which of the following will take place in the long run?

(A) Price decreases as more firms exit the market.
(B) Price decreases as more firms enter the market.
(C) Price increases as more firms enter the market.
(D) Profits decrease as price increases.
(E) none of the above

118. A movie theater offers tickets to the general public for $10. Students can buy tickets for $8. This is an example of

(A) dead weight loss
(B) variable costs
(C) price discrimination
(D) market power
(E) fixed costs

119. A monopoly refers to

(A) the least competitive market structure
(B) the most competitive market structure
(C) a market structure with a small number of interdependent large firms producing a standardized product
(D) extensive economies of scale and higher cost-efficiency when there is only one firm for the entire demand of a product
(E) the most competitive market structure

120. If prices fall below AVC, what should a firm decide to do?

(A) differentiate products
(B) raise prices
(C) cut TFC
(D) lay off workers
(E) shut down

121. The profit-maximizing rule states that to maximize profits a firm should produce where
    (A) MR = MC
    (B) MR > MC
    (C) MR < MC
    (D) MB > MC
    (E) MB = MC

122. When there is zero incentive for more firms to enter a perfectly competitive market, it is said that the market has reached
    (A) constant returns to scale
    (B) economies of scale
    (C) diseconomies of scale
    (D) long-run equilibrium
    (E) none of the above

123. If new firms enter the market, what is most likely to occur?
    (A) Total revenue will decrease.
    (B) Total revenue will increase.
    (C) Market power increases.
    (D) Market power decreases.
    (E) none of the above

124. Cartels are an example of
    (A) a perfect competition
    (B) a monopolistic competition
    (C) collusion
    (D) the best way to use dominant strategy
    (E) the prisoner's dilemma

125. Few large producers, barriers to entry, and mutual interdependence are characteristics of a(n)
    (A) perfect competition
    (B) monopolistic competition
    (C) oligopoly
    (D) monopoly
    (E) natural monopoly

126. Why is the demand for fruit less price elastic than the demand for a boat?

   (A) Consumption of fruit is greater.
   (B) A boat is an inferior good.
   (C) There are more suppliers of fruit than boat manufacturers.
   (D) Fruit takes up less of a consumer's budget.
   (E) all of the above

127. All of the following are long-run production decisions EXCEPT

   (A) an auto-repair shop decides to increase the size of its garage
   (B) a school decides to hire more teaching assistants due to an increase in the school population
   (C) a firm increases the number of its plants
   (D) a school decides to add more classrooms and a new performing arts center
   (E) a firm decides to close 5 percent of its plants

128. A perfect competition refers to

   (A) the most competitive market structure
   (B) the least competitive market structure
   (C) extensive economies of scale and higher cost-efficiency when there is only one firm for the entire demand of a product
   (D) a few small firms offering a differentiated product with easy entry into the market
   (E) a market structure with a small number of interdependent large firms producing a standardized product

129. The difference between a monopoly and a monopolistic competition is

   (A) differentiated products
   (B) economies of scale
   (C) long-term pricing power
   (D) government regulation
   (E) the size of the market

130. Firm X decides to shut down production in the short run where its costs would be

(A) AVC only
(B) AVC and TFC only
(C) TFC only
(D) zero
(E) none of the above

131. If a monopoly and a perfect competition have the same costs, the monopoly will always

(A) charge a lesser price than the perfect competition
(B) produce the same quantity as the perfect competition
(C) charge a higher price than the perfect competition and produce less
(D) charge a higher price than the perfect competition and produce more
(E) none of the above

132. No barriers to entry or exit, many firms, and a standardized product are characteristics of which type of market structure?

(A) monopolistic competition
(B) oligopoly
(C) natural monopoly
(D) monopoly
(E) perfect competition

133. The market for smartphones may be considered a monopolistic competition rather than a perfect competition because

(A) there is product differentiation
(B) there is no product differentiation
(C) profits in the long run decrease as more firms enter the market
(D) they are price takers
(E) all of the above

134. The services of natural gas, water, and electricity brought into the household are best consigned to which market structure?

(A) monopolistic competition
(B) oligopoly
(C) perfect competition
(D) natural monopoly
(E) monopoly

135. If the price of cigarettes, a normal good, is in equilibrium, which choice will result in a price increase for cigarettes?

(A) consumer income to decrease
(B) consumer expectations to remain the same
(C) the price of tobacco to increase
(D) the government to decrease regulations
(E) the price of tobacco to decrease

136. Consumer surplus is the

(A) difference between the price consumers would have been willing to pay and the price they actually did pay
(B) price consumers would have been willing to pay minus total variable costs
(C) price consumers would have been willing to pay in addition to total variable costs
(D) price consumers would have been willing to pay in addition to total fixed costs
(E) price consumers would have been willing to pay minus total fixed and variable costs

137. If you are reading a firm's business plan and see many resources dedicated to advertising, you would know that the firm's market structure is a(n)

(A) oligopoly
(B) natural monopoly
(C) monopoly
(D) perfect competition
(E) monopolistic competition

138. What is the most likely reason perfectly competitive firms do not make a profit in the long run?

(A) barriers of exit from the market
(B) the product being standardized with little differentiation
(C) the arrival of new firms on the market
(D) the firms being "price takers"
(E) all of the above

139. If firms are exiting a market and price is rising as a result, then

(A) there is a consumer shortage
(B) the market structure is a monopolistic competition
(C) P < ATC in a perfect competition
(D) P > ATC in a perfect competition
(E) P = ATC in a perfect competition

140. Which pricing and output choices would a monopolist select?

(A) Output should be MR = MC and P > MC.
(B) Output should be MR = MC and P = MC.
(C) Output should be MR > MC and P > MC.
(D) Output should be MR < MC and P > MC.
(E) Output should be MR = MC and P < TRC.

141. Which market structures have ease of entry and exit in the long run?

(A) perfect competition and monopoly
(B) perfect competition and monopolistic competition
(C) monopolistic competition and oligopoly
(D) oligopoly and natural monopoly
(E) all market structures

142. The government is needed to step in and regulate an electric natural monopoly. What must be done to ensure allocative efficiency?

(A) Regulate the natural monopoly to the point where P < MC.
(B) Regulate the natural monopoly to the point where P > MC.
(C) Regulate the natural monopoly to the point where P = MC.
(D) Regulate the natural monopoly to the point where P > TFC.
(E) none of the above

143. Marginal utility refers to

(A) the change in total utility as a result of the consumption of an additional unit of a good

(B) the change in a firm's total cost from hiring an additional unit of labor

(C) the change in saving caused by change in disposable income

(D) the additional cost of production for one more unit of output

(E) the additional cost incurred for the consumption of the next unit of a good

144. Peter loves French fries, and his friends dared him to eat nothing but French fries all day long. He greatly enjoyed eating 50 French fries, but when he consumed another 50 fries, he enjoyed them less and less because his stomach began to hurt. What does this scenario represent?

(A) marginal utility

(B) law of diminishing marginal utility

(C) MC = MB

(D) MB > MC

(E) A, B, and D

145. The key difference between accounting profit and economic profit is

(A) accounting profit includes the opportunity cost of capital

(B) economic profit includes the opportunity cost of capital

(C) economic profit is a key component of GDP

(D) economic profit is usually higher than accounting profit

(E) accounting profit is always higher than economic profit

Use the following graph to answer questions 146 and 147.

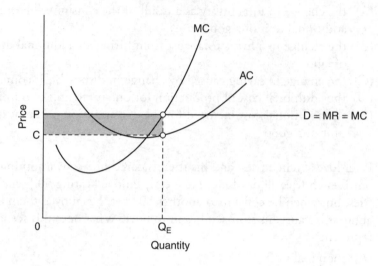

146. The diagram represents which type of market structure?

    (A) monopolistic competition
    (B) perfect competition
    (C) natural monopoly
    (D) monopoly
    (E) oligopoly

147. At which point is the graph showing profit maximization?

    (A) MR = MC
    (B) AC = P
    (C) MC = AC
    (D) the area between MC and AC
    (E) It is not showing profit maximization.

148. An airline may identify a specific group of people and charge them a different rate. This is known as

(A) a monopolistic competition
(B) price discrimination
(C) diseconomies of scale
(D) constant returns to scale
(E) illegal by current federal laws

149. Price discrimination might be successful if

(A) the firm can prevent resale to other consumers and identify and separate groups of consumers
(B) the firm does not have a monopoly on the pricing power of the good or service
(C) the firm has a monopoly on pricing power but cannot prevent resale to other consumers
(D) the firm does not have economies of scale
(E) the firm is operating within government regulations

150. Suppose you pick up the latest edition of *The Economist* and read that company Z, a producer of cigarettes, recently purchased 8 out of the 10 biggest farms that produce tobacco. Since you are a very good AP Economics student, you realize immediately that company Z is attempting to

(A) increase profits
(B) establish an oligopoly through collusive pricing
(C) maximize profits where marginal revenue equals marginal cost
(D) establish a monopoly through majority control of a factor of production
(E) none of the above

Use the following graph to answer question 151.

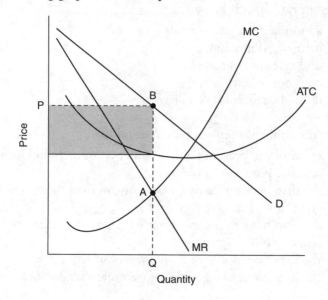

151. The graph represents a short-run monopolistic equilibrium. The shaded area represents

(A) surplus
(B) shortage
(C) profit
(D) price ceiling
(E) price floor

152. In the long run, monopolistically competitive firms break even due to

(A) government regulations
(B) price ceilings
(C) no entry or exit barriers
(D) exit of firms from the market
(E) non-price competition

153. Game theory fits best with which market structure?

  (A) monopolistic competition
  (B) perfect competition
  (C) monopoly
  (D) oligopoly
  (E) natural monopoly

154. The government establishes a price ceiling on good X above the equilibrium price. The result would

  (A) raise the price of the good
  (B) raise the price of the good and decrease the quantity demanded
  (C) lower the price of the good and increase the quantity demanded
  (D) lower the price of the good
  (E) have no effect on the price of the good or quantity demanded

Refer to the following graph for question 155.

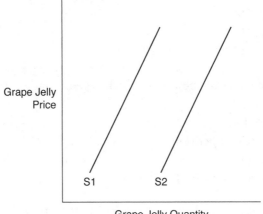

155. If peanut butter and grape jelly are complementary goods, and the supply of grape jelly moves from S1 to S2,

  (A) the demand curve for peanut butter will shift to the right
  (B) the demand curve for peanut butter will remain the same
  (C) the demand curve for peanut butter will shift to the left
  (D) quantity demanded will decrease for peanut butter on the same demand curve
  (E) quantity demanded will increase for peanut butter on the same demand curve

156. Which of the following shows the profit-maximizing point for all types of market structures?

(A) P < MC
(B) P = MC
(C) P = ATC
(D) P = MR
(E) MR = MC

157. In the market system, resources are allocated in which ways?

I. Customs and traditions influence which goods and services are produced.

II. Voluntary exchange influences which goods and services are produced.

III. Government determines which goods and services are produced.

(A) I only
(B) II only
(C) I and III
(D) I and II
(E) I, II, and III

158. Price leadership fits best with which type of market structure?

(A) monopoly
(B) natural monopoly
(C) perfect competition
(D) oligopoly
(E) monopolistic competition

159. The idea of limited liability is a significant factor to which type of business organization?

(A) sole proprietorships
(B) monopolies
(C) corporations
(D) partnerships
(E) all of the above

160. Implicit costs are

(A) direct, purchased, out-of-pocket costs
(B) costs that change with the level of output
(C) indirect costs or opportunity costs
(D) total variable costs divided by output
(E) none of the above

161. All of the following explain the downward slope of the demand curve EXCEPT

(A) income effect
(B) substitution effect
(C) diminishing marginal utility
(D) complement effect
(E) the relationship between marginal benefit and marginal cost

162. If an increase in technology in a perfectly competitive firm only lowers the firm's costs of production, what will the effect be?

	Price	Quantity	Profit
(A)	decrease	decrease	decrease
(B)	decrease	increase	increase
(C)	no change	decrease	increase
(D)	no change	increase	increase
(E)	increase	increase	increase

163. If tacos are a better substitute for burritos than hamburgers, tacos will have

(A) a higher cross-price elasticity of demand
(B) a lower cross-price elasticity of demand
(C) the same cross-price elasticity of demand
(D) a negative cross-price elasticity of demand
(E) a zero cross-price elasticity of demand

164. Measuring allocative efficiency through allocation of resources is best expressed in which formula?

(A) $P = MC$
(B) $P = AR$
(C) $MB > MC$
(D) $MB = MC$
(E) $P = ATC$

165. If corn oil is less substitutable for olive oil, then corn oil will have

(A) a higher cross-price elasticity of demand
(B) a lower cross-price elasticity of demand
(C) the same cross-price elasticity of demand
(D) a negative cross-price elasticity of demand
(E) an infinite cross-price elasticity of demand

166. If a cartel comes into existence, the most likely outcome would be that

(A) economic profits will be balanced among all cartel members
(B) each cartel member would attempt to cheat by producing more
(C) there is allocative efficiency
(D) prices will be established through the market forces of supply and demand
(E) advertising will push consumers to one firm or the other

167. Monopoly dead weight loss is caused by

(A) P > MC
(B) P = MC
(C) MC = MB
(D) MC > MB
(E) none of the above

168. If price equals marginal revenue, which equals marginal cost, which equals average total cost, all in the long run, what type of market structure would this be?

(A) monopolistic competition
(B) monopoly
(C) natural monopoly
(D) oligopoly
(E) perfect competition

169. All of the following are characteristic of an oligopoly EXCEPT

(A) price taking
(B) collusive behavior
(C) barriers to entry
(D) cheating on other firm members to produce more
(E) a few large firms

170. Which of the following is a significant factor in monopoly pricing power?

(A) barriers to entry
(B) advertising
(C) price discrimination
(D) no product differentiation
(E) all of the above

171. Price elasticity of demand is an extremely useful tool in economics because

(A) it indicates the equilibrium price
(B) it predicts the market forces of supply and demand
(C) it shows how consumer behavior is affected by price
(D) it predicts how much firms will produce until the shutdown point
(E) it indicates a balance between long-run and short-run production costs

172. If the government establishes a price less than the market equilibrium price, then it is a(n)

(A) effective price floor
(B) effective price ceiling
(C) barrier to entry
(D) barrier to exit
(E) none of the above

173. How do economists know that a good is a viable substitute?

(A) Calculate cross-elasticity and the result is a positive number.
(B) Calculate cross-elasticity and the result is a negative number.
(C) The product is price inelastic.
(D) Wait to see if the market forces of supply and demand balance to equilibrium for the potential substitute.
(E) none of the above

174. If economic profit is zero, then

(A) a firm earned a normal profit
(B) a firm did not earn an accounting profit
(C) a firm has reached its shutdown point in the short run
(D) a firm has reached its shutdown point in the long run
(E) a firm must lobby the government for assistance in subsidies

175. The freedom of entry and exit for a perfectly competitive market guarantees

(A) each firm knows how each other is planning its production

(B) no cheating on a firm's part to produce an additional unit of output

(C) economic profits will be zero in the long run

(D) economic profits will be greater than accounting profits

(E) economic profits will exceed marginal revenue

176. Producing to where MR = MC in a perfectly competitive market ensures

(A) the government will not intervene with regulations

(B) the ease of entry and exit in the market

(C) product differentiation

(D) earning an economic profit in the long run

(E) production efficiency in the long run

177. If a firm bases its decisions of pricing and production on the actions of other firms, then it is most likely a(n)

(A) monopolistic competition

(B) natural monopoly

(C) monopoly

(D) perfect competition

(E) oligopoly

178. A cartel will maximize profit when

(A) MC = MR

(B) MC < MR

(C) MC > MR

(D) W = MPR

(E) none of the above

179. The significant purpose of a "barrier to entry" in a market is

(A) it helps monopolies earn economic profit in the long run

(B) it restricts the creation of a cartel

(C) it restricts price discrimination

(D) it allows monopolistic competitive firms to differentiate their product

(E) it restricts collusive pricing practices

180. The income effect refers to

(A) the change in the quantity demanded due to a change in price of a relative good

(B) the change in the quantity demanded due to a change in a consumer's purchasing power

(C) the change in a consumer's total utility from the consumption of a good

(D) economic profits will be zero in the long run for a perfectly competitive market

(E) collusive pricing tactics that oligopolies use

181. Long-run profits for the perfectly competitive firm will always be

(A) greater than the marginal cost

(B) normal

(C) negative

(D) positive

(E) none of the above

Use the following graph to answer question 182.

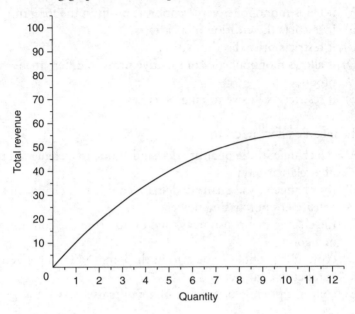

182. For the firm in this graph, marginal revenue is

    (A) constantly decreasing
    (B) constantly increasing
    (C) the same at every output level
    (D) increasing rapidly, then decreasing, then negative
    (E) increasing at a constant rate, then decreasing

183. Economies of scale

    (A) give large firms an advantage over smaller firms
    (B) give small firms an advantage over larger firms
    (C) increase production costs
    (D) result in lower profits
    (E) are the same as diseconomies of scale

184. The price of a golf ball increases from $1 to $1.25. As a result, golf ball sales fall by 50 percent. Demand for golf balls is

(A) inelastic

(B) perfectly inelastic

(C) elastic

(D) perfectly elastic

(E) neither elastic nor inelastic

185. If P = ATC, then

(A) economic profit is zero

(B) accounting profit is zero

(C) normal profit is unattainable

(D) firms are operating inefficiently

(E) all of the above

186. Since the monopolist has many barriers to entry and no competition, he or she has price-setting ability. This is also known as

(A) purchasing power

(B) profit maximization

(C) market power

(D) efficiency

(E) none of the above

187. Firms engaged in a monopolistically competitive market have some market power because

(A) the firms have few competitors

(B) the firms have differentiated products

(C) the government restricts the use of patents for the firms through antitrust legislation

(D) advertising allows the firms to set any price they wish

(E) none of the above

188. Imagine a perfectly competitive market. If the market price of the product is $15 and the marginal cost is also $15, which of the following is true?

(A) The firm is making zero profit.

(B) Many firms will soon leave the market.

(C) Many firms will join together to increase profit through collusive pricing.

(D) The firm is profit maximizing.

(E) all of the above

189. For a perfectly competitive market, the best way to maximize profit is

(A) MR = MC

(B) MRP < W

(C) AFC = MB

(D) MC > MB

(E) none of the above

190. When the government grants a patent to a firm, the market for the patented product becomes a(n)

(A) monopoly

(B) oligopoly

(C) cartel

(D) monopolistic competition

(E) pure competition

191. Economies of scale refers to

(A) an increase in ATC as quantity increases

(B) a decrease in ATC as quantity increases

(C) a decrease in ATC as quantity decreases

(D) a firm maximizing profit through dominance of the market

(E) sensitivity to the determinants of supply and demand and price level

192. The federal government increases mass transit subsidies, and as a result, the price of a train ticket from New York to Boston decreases by 40 percent. Ridership increases from 10 million to 12 million as a result. Demand for train tickets is

(A) inelastic
(B) perfectly inelastic
(C) elastic
(D) perfectly elastic
(E) neither elastic nor inelastic

193. A bank accepts $10 in quarters in exchange for a $10 bill. If it asks for more than $10 in quarters for a $10 bill, consumers will not accept the exchange offer. Demand for the exchange service is

(A) inelastic
(B) perfectly inelastic
(C) elastic
(D) perfectly elastic
(E) neither elastic nor inelastic

194. A handbag designer sells luxury handbags for $2,000. The designer raises the handbag price to $4,000 and demand for handbags increases 50 percent. What type of good is a handbag?

(A) a Giffen good
(B) a Veblen good
(C) an inferior good
(D) a substitute good
(E) a factor of production

195. A worker at a shoe store buys five pounds of rice, which is less expensive than other food items, each week. The rice farm increases the price of rice and the shoe store worker starts buying six pounds of rice each week. What type of good is the rice?

(A) a Veblen good
(B) a normal good
(C) a substitute good
(D) a Giffen good
(E) a luxury good

196. Firm A and firm B offer high-speed Internet service. When firm B increases the price of its Internet service by 20 percent, people stop purchasing Internet service from firm B. In comparison with firm B's Internet service, firm A's Internet service is a(n)

(A) complementary good
(B) perfect substitute
(C) imperfect substitute
(D) public good
(E) inferior good

197. A 20 percent increase in gasoline prices does not affect demand in the next week, but in the next month the quantity of gasoline demanded falls 10 percent. Which factor affected the price elasticity of gasoline?

(A) duration
(B) brand loyalty
(C) the income effect
(D) conspicuous consumption
(E) breadth of definition of the good

Use the following graph to answer questions 198 and 199.

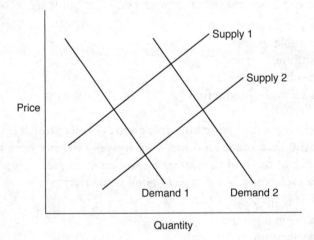

198. What factor would NOT contribute to a shift from Demand 2 to Demand 1?

(A) The product becomes less popular.

(B) A substitute product leaves the market.

(C) A recession reduces consumer income.

(D) Researchers discover the product's health risks.

(E) A substitute product enters the market.

199. What factors would contribute to a shift from Supply 1 to Supply 2?

(A) A key production input becomes less expensive.

(B) The factory becomes more efficient at producing this product.

(C) Production workers' wages decrease.

(D) The government reduces taxes on the factory.

(E) All of these factors would shift supply from S1 to S2.

200. The government guarantees farmers will receive a certain price for their crops. What does this represent?

(A) a shortage

(B) a price ceiling

(C) a price floor

(D) an increase in the equilibrium price

(E) an increase in the equilibrium quantity

201. A restaurant just learned that a conference will attract many potential customers to its city in the next month. Which choice would NOT increase revenue in the short term?

(A) hire more kitchen staff

(B) buy more cooking ingredients

(C) expand the size of its dining facility

(D) buy more plates and dishes

(E) spend more money on ads

Use the following graph of rental prices and rental quantity to answer questions 202 and 203.

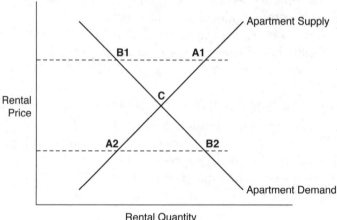

202. What moves on the apartment supply and demand curves would represent the passage of rent control laws that limited the maximum apartment rental price?

(A) Apartments supplied would move to A2 and apartments demanded would move to B2.

(B) Apartments supplied would move to A1 and apartments demanded would move to B1.

(C) Apartments supplied would move to A1 and apartments demanded would move to B2.

(D) Apartments supplied would move to A2 and apartments demanded would move to B1.

(E) Apartments supplied would be equal to apartments demanded at point C.

203. A shortage of rental apartments would result in a dead weight loss. Which area would represent the value of this loss?

(A) the area between points A2, B2, and C

(B) the area between points B1, C, and A2

(C) the area between points B1, C, and A1

(D) the area between points A1, C, and B2

(E) not enough information available to answer this question

Refer to the following graph, which reflects the market for a soda manufacturer, to answer questions 204–206.

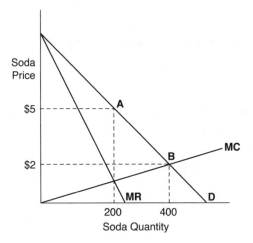

204. What is the soda manufacturer's economic profit if it has a monopoly?

(A) $800
(B) $1,000
(C) $400
(D) $600
(E) $0

205. Which areas on the chart reflect the dead weight loss caused by the monopoly?

(A) the triangle bounded by points A, B, and (200, $2)
(B) the triangle bounded by points A, B, and (200, $2) AND the triangle bounded by point B, ($2, 200), and the point where MR = MC
(C) the rectangle containing point A and (0, $2)
(D) the rectangle containing point A and (0, $0)
(E) the triangle containing the area between D and MR but above MC

206. If the soda price and quantity shifted from point A to point B, this would indicate

    (A) demand for soda increased
    (B) economies of scale
    (C) other soda manufacturers entered the market
    (D) decreased price competition
    (E) diseconomies of scale

207. A tire factory buys rubber to make tires. The price of rubber declines. As a result,

    (A) marginal cost decreases
    (B) fixed cost decreases
    (C) average total cost increases
    (D) average fixed cost decreases
    (E) fixed cost increases

208. Joe resigned from his engineering job, where he earned $50,000, to open a restaurant. He earns a profit of $40,000 as the restaurant owner. As the restaurant owner, Joe earns

    (A) a normal profit
    (B) an economic profit
    (C) an accounting profit
    (D) an abnormal profit
    (E) both B and C

209. Jeff opens a shoe store. He earns $50,000 in the first year, but his profit falls to $30,000 in the second year after more shoe stores open up in town. He would earn $30,000 if he worked for another firm as an employee. In the second year, the shoe store has reached

    (A) economic profit
    (B) short-run equilibrium
    (C) long-run equilibrium
    (D) market surplus
    (E) dead weight loss

210. A furniture company opens up a plant and earns a profit of $50,000 from the plant. After it opens up a second plant, doubling production quantity, the first and second plants each earn the furniture company $60,000 in profit. The furniture company achieved

(A) diseconomies of scale
(B) economies of scale
(C) diminishing marginal returns
(D) a monopoly
(E) perfect competition

211. An auto manufacturer earns a profit of $100,000 from its plant. It opens up second and third plants, tripling production quantity, and profit rises to $300,000. This indicates

(A) economies of scale
(B) diseconomies of scale
(C) constant returns to scale
(D) diminishing marginal returns
(E) monopolistic competition

212. Competition in a market system best helps a society because

(A) supply and demand establish the best price for a good or service
(B) all opportunity costs are heavily analyzed
(C) the total welfare is increased
(D) aggregate supply and aggregate demand are balanced
(E) within the production possibilities frontier, all resources are maximized and used efficiently

213. An auto parts manufacturer starts buying large quantities of steel, reducing its variable cost per unit. It also begins to specialize in car door production instead of manufacturing every part of the car. As a result, production increases and average cost decreases. The auto parts manufacturer achieved

(A) economies of scale
(B) diseconomies of scale
(C) short-run equilibrium
(D) declining returns to scale
(E) constant returns to scale

214. Bill leaves his job as a lawyer to open up a clothing store. He earned $100,000 as a lawyer and earns $120,000 as owner of the clothing store. His economic profit is

(A) $120,000
(B) $100,000
(C) $20,000
(D) $0
(E) $220,000

215. A few laptop manufacturers are competing in a market. The laptops have slightly different styles and similar prices. The laptop manufacturers earn economic profits in the long run. The market is a(n)

(A) oligopoly
(B) monopoly
(C) perfect competition
(D) monopolistic competition
(E) none of the above

216. Nate opens up a restaurant and earns a profit of $60,000 per year. He is offered a job as a factory manager paying $80,000 per year. His economic profit is

(A) –$20,000
(B) $80,000
(C) –$80,000
(D) $0
(E) $140,000

217. If the demand curve remains constant, and supply decreases, the result will be

(A) a decrease in prices and a larger quantity sold
(B) an increase in prices and a smaller quantity sold
(C) a decrease in prices and a smaller quantity sold
(D) an increase in prices and a larger quantity sold
(E) none of the above

218. Several oil companies form an industry organization that sets the price of a barrel of oil. This is NOT

(A) a monopoly
(B) a cartel
(C) collusion
(D) an oligopoly
(E) market power

219. An agricultural community has four banana farms, five plum farms, six grape farms, and seven apple farms. Demand is likely the MOST price elastic for which fruit?

(A) apples
(B) bananas
(C) plums
(D) grapes
(E) not enough information

220. Many farms are selling peanuts. The peanuts are not differentiated and the peanut farms are not earning an economic profit. Demand for a peanut farm is likely

(A) elastic
(B) perfectly elastic
(C) inelastic
(D) perfectly inelastic
(E) downward sloping

221. An auto manufacturer needs to reduce costs in the short run. It can make any of these decisions EXCEPT

(A) lay off 10 percent of the auto workers
(B) shut down 5 percent of its plants
(C) order smaller quantities of metal and rubber
(D) shut down a production line
(E) refinance corporate bonds

222. A price increase in product B resulted in a price increase for product C. Product C is most likely a(n)

(A) inferior good
(B) complementary good
(C) normal good
(D) substitute good
(E) factor of production

223. A toy manufacturer adds an employee and average cost decreases. It continues to add more employees. At first, average cost decreases even further, but with even more employees average cost begins to rise. This reflects

(A) economies of scale
(B) diseconomies of scale
(C) constant economies of scale
(D) the U-shaped average cost curve
(E) new firms entering the market

224. A group of truck manufacturers are competing in a market. The trucks they manufacture are differentiated products. If this market is an oligopoly and NOT a monopolistic competition,

(A) truck manufacturers must consider other firms' responses when making business decisions
(B) the trucks would not be differentiated
(C) there would be many truck manufacturers
(D) truck manufacturers would have no incentive to collude
(E) truck manufacturers would have market power

225. An auto parts manufacturer has fixed costs of $40,000. It can shut down or produce tires at a loss of $10,000. If it decides to produce tires, its economic profit is

(A) −$10,000
(B) $40,000
(C) $30,000
(D) $50,000
(E) −$30,000

226. Four cable companies have 90 percent market share. These firms may be

(A) price takers
(B) in collusion
(C) in perfect competition
(D) unconcerned with other cable companies' pricing strategies
(E) earning a normal profit in the long run

227. Many small potato farms are growing potatoes. Three large French fry manufacturers are buying all of the potatoes. The potato market is best described as

(A) perfect competition
(B) an oligopoly
(C) an oligopsony
(D) a monopsony
(E) monopolistic competition

228. When a steel manufacturer is buying all of the iron ore produced by many mines, it is likely

(A) a price taker
(B) a monopsony
(C) not insulated from supply and demand fluctuations
(D) at a negotiating disadvantage to suppliers
(E) engaged in perfect competition

229. A movie studio charges $8 to watch one of its films over the Internet in the United States, and $12 to watch the film from Australia. This is an example of

(A) collusion
(B) price discrimination
(C) economies of scale
(D) a cartel
(E) game theory

The following table illustrates choices available to firm A and firm B. Use this table to answer questions 230 and 231.

		Raise Price **Firm A**	Lower Price
	Raise Price	$10, $10	$25, –$5
Firm B			
	Lower Price	–$5, $25	$0, $0

230. Using the table, what decision would result in the best outcome for firm A?

(A) Firm A lowers prices and firm B raises prices.
(B) Firm B lowers prices and firm A raises prices.
(C) Firms A and B both raise prices.
(D) Firms A and B both lower prices.
(E) none of the above

231. What outcome would be best for both firms?

(A) Firm A raises prices and firm B raises prices.
(B) Firm A lowers prices and firm B raises prices.
(C) Firm A raises prices and firm B lowers prices.
(D) Firm A lowers prices and firm B lowers prices.
(E) none of the above

232. In which type of market would a firm use a payoff matrix to set pricing policy?

(A) a monopoly
(B) perfect competition
(C) monopolistic competition
(D) oligopoly
(E) natural monopoly

233. If Firm A and firm B are in a prisoner's dilemma situation, the Nash equilibrium is
(A) Firm A defects and firm B defects
(B) Firm A cooperates and firm B defects
(C) Firm A defects and firm B cooperates
(D) Firm A cooperates and firm B cooperates
(E) none of the above

234. A group of oil producers have formed a cartel. The cartel is restricting quantity supplied to set a higher price for oil. To maximize its profit, an individual oil producer should
(A) raise the price of its oil
(B) lower the price of its oil
(C) increase quantity supplied for its oil
(D) decrease quantity supplied for its oil
(E) leave the oil price and quantity supplied unchanged

This table illustrates choices available to Betty's and Joey's, two restaurants. Refer to this table for questions 235 and 236.

	Don't Buy **Joey's**	Buy Ads
Don't Buy **Betty's**	$50, $50	$70, $30
Buy Ads	$30, $70	$40, $40

235. What is the dominant strategy for Joey's?
(A) don't buy ads no matter what happens
(B) buy ads only if Betty's buys ads
(C) don't buy ads if Betty's buys ads
(D) buy ads no matter what happens
(E) none of the above

236. What choice results in the lowest profit for Betty's and Joey's?

(A) Joey's buys ads and Betty's buys ads.

(B) Joey's buys ads and Betty's does not buy ads.

(C) Joey's does not buy ads and Betty's does not buy ads.

(D) Joey's does not buy ads and Betty's buys ads.

(E) none of the above

237. Max quit his job as an economics professor earning $100,000 a year to open up a bakery. He also invested $50,000 in the bakery, money that had been earning him $5,000 per year in dividends. The bakery earned $120,000 in its first year. What was Max's economic profit?

(A) $120,000

(B) $20,000

(C) $15,000

(D) $115,000

(E) –$50,000

238. The price of sugar is currently $3 per pound. The government establishes a price floor at $2 per pound. What happens to sugar supply?

(A) There will be an oversupply of sugar.

(B) Quantity demanded will equal quantity supplied.

(C) There will be an undersupply of sugar.

(D) The supply curve for sugar will shift to the left.

(E) The supply curve for sugar will shift to the right.

239. Producer surplus is equal to

(A) the area to the left of the demand curve and below the price equilibrium

(B) the area to the right of the demand curve and below the price equilibrium

(C) the area to the left of the demand curve and above the price equilibrium

(D) the area to the right of the demand curve and above the price equilibrium

(E) the area to the right of the supply curve and to the left of the demand curve

Refer to the following graph for questions 240 and 241.

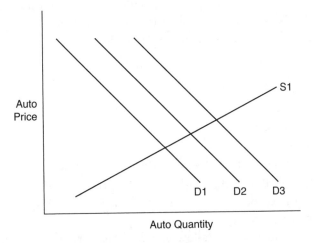

240. If auto demand shifted from D2 to D1 because of consumer expectations, what could this indicate?

(A) Consumers expect auto prices to fall.
(B) Consumers expect auto prices to rise.
(C) Consumers expect auto prices to stay the same.
(D) Consumers expect an economic expansion.
(E) Consumers expect raw materials costs for autos to increase.

241. Which demand shift would indicate that consumers expect higher auto prices?

(A) from D2 to D1
(B) from D3 to D2
(C) from D1 to D3
(D) from D3 to D1
(E) none of the above

242. A group of farms includes chicken, pork, fish, and steak producers. Chicken is a substitute good for pork, and pork is a substitute good for fish. No product is a substitute good for steak. Demand is likely the LEAST price elastic for which product?

(A) chicken
(B) pork
(C) fish
(D) steak
(E) not enough information

243. If P < ATC in a market with perfect competition,

(A) firms will exit the market and the price will rise
(B) high exit barriers will prevent firms from leaving and the price will not change
(C) low entry barriers allow new firms to enter the market and the price will fall
(D) firms will not enter or exit the market because it is at long-run equilibrium
(E) none of the above

244. A movie theater chain owns all of the theaters in a city. It sells movie tickets for $12. To reduce dead weight loss, the theater chain should

(A) raise the ticket price to $15
(B) hire more employees
(C) offer matinee showings for $6
(D) close some of its theaters
(E) open restaurants at its theaters

245. An auto manufacturer has an output level where the marginal cost of a car is $20,000 and the marginal revenue from a car is $20,000. To maximize its profit, the auto manufacturer should

(A) keep output the same
(B) increase output
(C) reduce output
(D) increase the price
(E) reduce the price

246. An automaker is willing to sell a car for $30,000. A consumer is willing to buy a car for $50,000. The equilibrium price for cars in the market is $40,000. Producer surplus is

(A) $30,000
(B) $20,000
(C) $40,000
(D) $10,000
(E) $50,000

247. A banana farm will sell a banana for $2. A consumer will pay $2.60 for the banana. The market price of a banana is $2.25. Consumer surplus is

(A) $2.00
(B) $2.25
(C) $2.60
(D) $0.25
(E) $0.35

248. A raspberry farm is selling boxes of raspberries. At the current output level, a box has a marginal cost of $4. Marginal cost would equal marginal revenue at $5. At this output level, a box of raspberries would sell for $6 on the market. The raspberry farm should

(A) increase raspberry output until marginal cost is $5
(B) increase raspberry output until marginal cost is $6
(C) shut down
(D) keep raspberry output the same
(E) lower raspberry output

249. A cloud hosting company has a monopoly and wants to increase its profits. The company should

(A) acquire patents from other firms
(B) cut prices on all of its hosting services
(C) create different pricing tiers for businesses and consumers
(D) increase prices on all of its hosting services
(E) bundle its hosting services with tax preparation software

250. A cruise line provides all of the cruises in its market. It sells cruise tickets for $1,000. If it introduces senior tickets for $800,

(A) the cruise line's profit will increase
(B) the cruise line's profit will decrease
(C) dead weight loss will increase
(D) quantity supplied will decrease
(E) the cruise line will earn a normal profit

251. A group of four auto manufacturers has 80 percent market share. This could be because of

(A) low construction costs for an auto plant
(B) patents on auto parts
(C) auto manufacturers deciding not to collude
(D) normal long-run profit
(E) few economies of scale

252. An auto parts manufacturer decides to produce car doors worth $80,000. It could have produced car windows worth $60,000 instead. Its implicit costs were

(A) $20,000
(B) $60,000
(C) $80,000
(D) $0
(E) $140,000

253. A department store bought a plot of land for $50,000 and built a store on the land three decades ago. Today, a grocery store offers to buy the land for $1 million. If the department store turns down the offer, the implicit cost of the land is

(A) $50,000
(B) $950,000
(C) $1 million
(D) $0
(E) $1,050,000

254. A restaurant chain owns the land underneath one of its restaurants. This property earns an accounting profit of $100,000 per year. The restaurant chain could earn $120,000 per year if it rented out the property instead. To earn a normal profit, the accounting profit from this property must increase by

(A) $100,000
(B) $20,000
(C) –$20,000
(D) $120,000
(E) $0

255. If firms in a market are utilizing their resources to allocative efficiency, the market is a(n)

(A) perfect competition
(B) monopolistic competition
(C) monopoly
(D) oligopoly
(E) natural monopoly

256. When a government establishes an intervention price and the price moves below this level,

(A) producer surplus decreases
(B) the demand curve shifts to the right
(C) the supply curve shifts to the left
(D) the equilibrium point shifts to the left
(E) consumer surplus increases

257. If the tomato price increases by 20 percent, and as a result quantity demanded for lettuce increases by 40 percent, the cross-price elasticity of demand for tomatoes and lettuce is

(A) 2
(B) 0.5
(C) –2
(D) 0.5
(E) 0

258. Peanut butter and blackberry jam have a cross-price demand elasticity of –2. The price of peanut butter increases by 20 percent. As a result, quantity demanded for blackberry jam will

(A) fall 20 percent
(B) fall 40 percent
(C) rise 20 percent
(D) rise 40 percent
(E) remain the same

Use the following graph to answer questions 259 and 260.

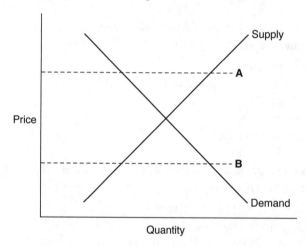

259. Which area represents a surplus created by a price floor?

(A) the area below line A and between the supply and demand curves
(B) the area above line B and between the supply and demand curves
(C) the area above line A and to the right of the supply curve
(D) the area below line B and to the right of the demand curve
(E) the area above line A and between the supply and demand curves

260. Which area represents a shortage caused by a price ceiling?

    (A) the area underneath line A and between the supply and demand curves

    (B) the area above line B and between the supply and demand curves

    (C) the area above line A and to the right of the supply curve

    (D) the area below line B and to the right of the demand curve

    (E) the area below line B and between the supply and demand curves

261. Quantity demanded for pork is 10. The price of chicken increases 10 percent. If pork and chicken have a cross-price elasticity of 5, the new quantity demanded for pork will be

    (A) 10

    (B) 15

    (C) 2

    (D) 5

    (E) 50

262. The price of bread increases by 50 percent. As a result, quantity demanded for cheese falls 20 percent. The cross-price elasticity of demand for bread and cheese is

    (A) 0.4

    (B) −0.4

    (C) 2.5

    (D) −2.5

    (E) 1

263. Cross-price elasticity for corn and wheat is 0.75. The corn price rises 40 percent. As a result, the new quantity demanded for wheat is 13. What was quantity demanded for wheat before the corn price increased?

    (A) 16

    (B) 17.5

    (C) 10

    (D) 8

    (E) 7.5

264. The price of peaches increases 30 percent. As a result, quantity demanded for plums increases from 50 to 80. What is the price elasticity of demand for peaches and plums?

(A) 2
(B) –2
(C) 0.5
(D) –0.5
(E) 1

265. The price of a truck increases from $70,000 to $77,000. As a result, quantity demanded for radios falls 30 percent. The price elasticity of demand for trucks and radios is

(A) 3
(B) –3
(C) 0.33
(D) –0.33
(E) 0

266. If the price of grapes rises 20 percent, and as a result quantity demanded for bananas rises 5 percent, the cross-price elasticity of demand for grapes and bananas is

(A) 4
(B) –4
(C) 0.25
(D) –0.25
(E) 0

267. If the price of grapes increases 10 percent, and the quantity supplied for grapes increases 30 percent, the price elasticity of supply for grapes is

(A) 3
(B) –3
(C) 0.33
(D) –0.33
(E) 0

268. If apple prices increase 20 percent, and quantity supplied for apples increases 20 percent, then price elasticity of supply for apples is

(A) perfectly elastic
(B) perfectly inelastic
(C) elastic
(D) inelastic
(E) unitary elastic

269. If the price of bananas increases 30 percent, but quantity supplied for bananas does NOT change, supply is

(A) perfectly elastic
(B) perfectly inelastic
(C) elastic
(D) inelastic
(E) unitary elastic

270. If a sandwich shop can hire workers easily and the job does not require much training, sandwich ingredients are widely available and used by other industries, and lots of retail space is available, price elasticity of supply for sandwiches is likely to be

(A) greater than 1
(B) equal to 1
(C) less than 1
(D) zero
(E) negative

271. If the price elasticity of demand for bananas is 2 in the short run, over the long run it is likely that price elasticity of demand for bananas will be

(A) less than 2
(B) more than 2
(C) equal to 2
(D) less than 1
(E) zero

272. The price of a bell pepper increases from $1 to $1.20. Quantity supplied for bell peppers increases from 40 to 60. Price elasticity of supply for bell peppers is
    (A) 2.5
    (B) 1.5
    (C) 2.0
    (D) 0.2
    (E) 0.5

273. The price of a peach falls from $2 to $1.40. Quantity supplied for peaches falls from 100 to 85. Price elasticity of supply for peaches is
    (A) −0.5
    (B) 2
    (C) 0.3
    (D) 0.15
    (E) 0.5

274. A fashion retailer can easily order new inventory and can employ inexperienced workers in its stores. A motorcycle manufacturer must wait several months for part shipments and workers need training to work at the motorcycle plant. Price elasticity of supply for the fashion retailer and the motorcycle manufacturer, respectively, are likely to be
    (A) high, high
    (B) high, low
    (C) low, high
    (D) low, low
    (E) not enough information provided

275. If the price of a good decreases, the most likely result would be for the

(A) quantity supplied to increase
(B) quantity supplied to decrease
(C) demand to increase
(D) supply to decrease
(E) demand to decrease

276. If a nation's income increases by 5 percent and quantity demanded for sports cars rises by 15 percent, income elasticity of demand for sports cars is

(A) 3
(B) −3
(C) 0.33
(D) −0.33
(E) 0.5

277. If consumers demand more soda, but health care costs increase as well, this indicates a

(A) negative externality
(B) price ceiling
(C) price support
(D) price floor
(E) decrease in production costs

278. The number of buyers in a market, consumer tastes, the availability of substitute goods, and income are known as

(A) factors of supply
(B) determinants of demand
(C) consumer expectations
(D) factors of production
(E) marginal benefits

Refer to the following graph for question 279.

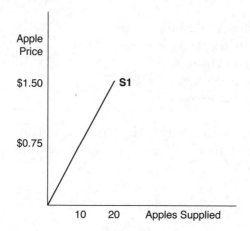

279. What is the price elasticity of supply for apples?

(A) 1
(B) 0.5
(C) 2
(D) 1.5
(E) 7.5

280. German consumers experience a 30 percent income rise. Quantity demanded for oatmeal falls 15 percent in Germany. Income elasticity of demand for oatmeal is

(A) 0.3
(B) 0.5
(C) –0.5
(D) 2
(E) –2

281. Income for New York consumers rises 20 percent. Quantity demanded for heating oil doesn't change. Heating oil is a

(A) sticky good
(B) inferior good
(C) luxury good
(D) normal good
(E) necessity good

282. The government imposes a $50 tax on television sets. Price elasticity of supply for television sets is 0.6 and price elasticity of demand for television sets is −0.2. As a result of the tax increase, a consumer who buys a television set will pay an additional

(A) $50
(B) $0
(C) $37.50
(D) $25
(E) $12

283. The government places a tariff on imported cars. If price elasticity of supply for cars is 0.6, and price elasticity of demand for cars is −0.4, what percentage of the tariff is paid by the car buyer?

(A) 100 percent
(B) 60 percent
(C) 40 percent
(D) 20 percent
(E) 0 percent

284. If the government raises taxes on lawnmowers, and lawnmower manufacturers do not increase the price of lawnmowers, then

(A) lawnmower supply is inelastic and lawnmower demand is inelastic
(B) lawnmower supply is inelastic and lawnmower demand is elastic
(C) lawnmower supply is elastic and lawnmower demand is inelastic
(D) lawnmower supply is elastic and lawnmower demand is elastic
(E) none of the above

285. If the government raises prices on autos, and auto manufacturers pass the entire cost of the tax to auto buyers, then

(A) auto supply is inelastic and auto demand is inelastic
(B) auto supply is inelastic and auto demand is elastic
(C) auto supply is elastic and auto demand is inelastic
(D) auto supply is elastic and auto demand is elastic
(E) none of the above

286. The government requires tomato growers to pay medical benefits for farm workers. This increases the cost of growing a tomato by 20 percent. If price elasticity of supply for tomatoes is 0.4 and price elasticity of demand for tomatoes is –0.6, the price of a tomato will rise by

(A) 20 percent
(B) 12 percent
(C) 8 percent
(D) 40 percent
(E) 16 percent

287. The government places a 30 percent tariff on imported clothing, which is sold to consumers by clothing stores. Price elasticity of supply for clothing is 0.9 and price elasticity of demand for clothing is –0.3. As a result of the tariff, clothing stores absorb a cost increase of

(A) 25 percent
(B) 75 percent
(C) 30 percent
(D) 7.5 percent
(E) 15 percent

288. Which factor would allow a manufacturer to pass on more of a tax increase to buyers?

(A) difficulty in changing production levels
(B) wide availability of substitute goods
(C) difficulty in moving the factory to another location
(D) the good is a necessity
(E) the good is a luxury item

289. The government raises the tax on a truck by $10,000. The price elasticity of supply for trucks is 1.5 and the price elasticity of demand is –1.0. Truck manufacturers will absorb costs of

(A) $10,000
(B) $6,000
(C) $4,000
(D) $2,000
(E) $0

290. The government places a tax on bicycle manufacturers. Bicycle supply is inelastic and demand is elastic. A possible response by bicycle manufacturers would be

(A) raise bicycle prices
(B) pass the tax hike to bicycle buyers
(C) reduce wages at the bicycle manufacturing plant
(D) reduce bicycle prices
(E) hire more employees

The following graph represents consumer indifference curves and is used for questions 291 and 292.

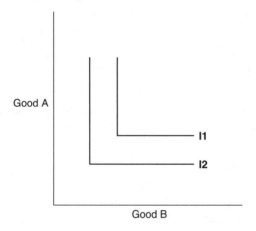

291. Good A and good B are

(A) normal goods
(B) perfect complements
(C) substitute goods
(D) inferior goods
(E) perfect substitutes

292. Good A and good B could represent

(A) a shirt and a pair of pants
(B) a left sandal and a right sandal
(C) a hat and a coat
(D) a loaf of bread and a bottle of water
(E) a potato and a banana

The following graph represents consumer indifference curves and is used for questions 293 and 294.

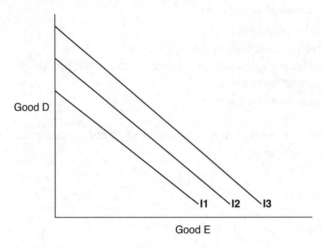

293. If consumption moves from indifference curve I2 to curve I3, this would indicate a(n)

(A) economic recession
(B) increase in supply
(C) preference for good D over good E
(D) preference for good E over good D
(E) rise in consumer income

294. Good D and good E are

(A) perfect complements
(B) perfect substitutes
(C) substitute goods
(D) complementary goods
(E) Giffen goods

295. A consumer's indifference curve is typically convex because of

(A) decreasing marginal utility
(B) increasing marginal utility
(C) satiation
(D) the bliss point
(E) a lack of budget constraints

The following graph represents consumer indifference curves and is used for questions 296 and 297.

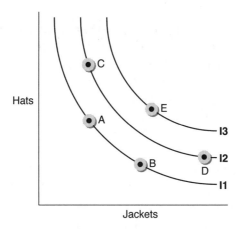

296. A consumer would be equally satisfied with the amount of hats and jackets available at
    (A) point A and point D
    (B) point B and point D
    (C) point B and point E
    (D) point C and point D
    (E) point C and point E

297. Economic expansion could result in a shift in consumer preferences from
    (A) point A to point B
    (B) point C to point D
    (C) point D to point E
    (D) point B to point A
    (E) point D to point C

298. A consumer indifference curve shows consumption preferences for goods A and B, which are both normal goods. If the price of good A decreases,

(A) consumption shifts to an indifference curve on the right

(B) consumption shifts to an indifference curve on the left

(C) quantity demanded increases for good A and consumption remains on the same curve

(D) quantity demanded decreases for good A and consumption remains on the same curve

(E) none of the above

299. Consumption shifts to an indifference curve on the left. Quantity demanded increases for good A and decreases for good B. This indicates that

(A) good A is a normal good and good B is an inferior good

(B) good A is an inferior good and good B is a normal good

(C) good A and good B are both normal goods

(D) good A and good B are both inferior goods

(E) good A is a luxury good

300. A consumer indifference curve shows consumption preferences for goods C and D, which are both normal goods. If the price of good D increases,

(A) consumption shifts to an indifference curve on the left

(B) consumption shifts to an indifference curve on the right

(C) quantity demanded decreases for good D and consumption remains on the same curve

(D) quantity demanded increases for good D and consumption remains on the same curve

(E) none of the above

301. If a consumer indifference curve shows consumption preferences for good A and good B, equilibrium consumption for these goods is located

(A) at the point where the budget constraint line is tangent to the consumer indifference curve
(B) at any point on the consumer indifference curve
(C) at any point on the budget constraint line
(D) at the point where the budget constraint line crosses the consumer indifference curve
(E) none of the above

The following graph shows a consumer indifference curve and demand for rice and lentils. Refer to it for question 302.

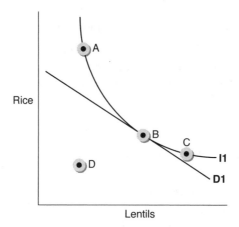

302. Equilibrium consumption for rice and lentils is located at

(A) point A
(B) point B
(C) point C
(D) point D
(E) none of the above

303. Excess demand is also known as

(A) shortage
(B) tariff
(C) price fixing
(D) surplus
(E) marginal cost

304. The substitution effect states that as the price of a good falls,

(A) it becomes more expensive in comparison with other goods
(B) it becomes less expensive in comparison with other goods
(C) consumers gain more buying power
(D) consumers lose buying power
(E) consumer income rises

305. The income effect states that as the price of a good falls,

(A) it becomes more expensive in comparison with other goods
(B) it becomes less expensive in comparison with other goods
(C) consumers gain more buying power
(D) consumers lose buying power
(E) consumer income rises

306. The demand curve for a private good is

(A) the horizontal sum of each consumer's demand curve
(B) the vertical sum of each consumer's demand curve
(C) the product of each consumer's demand curve
(D) the quotient of each consumer's demand curve
(E) none of the above

307. Establishing an effective price ceiling would

(A) create a market shortage
(B) eliminate a market shortage
(C) reduce demand
(D) reduce quantity demanded
(E) increase supply

308. Quantity demanded for cars would fall, but demand for cars would remain the same, if

(A) the price of gasoline rose
(B) trucks became more popular compared to cars
(C) a rise in auto accidents made consumers worried about car safety
(D) car manufacturers left the market
(E) bus fare decreased so fewer people drove cars to work

309. Quantity demanded for sugar beets would increase, but demand for sugar beets would remain the same, if

(A) researchers discovered that an artificial sweetener had health risks
(B) consumers switched to regular soda instead of diet soda
(C) more farmers began growing sugar beets
(D) a trade embargo reduced the supply of cane sugar
(E) sugar beets became a biofuel feedstock

310. The number of buyers in the market and the number of producers in the market are

(A) determinants of elasticity
(B) determinants of demand
(C) determinants of supply
(D) determined by the government in a market economy
(E) determined by the factors of production

311. Quantity supplied for mushrooms would increase, but supply for mushrooms would remain the same, if

(A) more farms began growing mushrooms
(B) a research study highlighted the health benefits of mushrooms
(C) the price of fertilizer, a production input, declined
(D) the government granted a tax credit to mushroom farmers
(E) a new type of tractor made mushroom farmers more efficient

312. Quantity supplied for strawberries would decrease, but supply for strawberries would remain the same, if

(A) wages for farm workers rose
(B) strawberry farms experienced a drought
(C) consumer income falls
(D) strawberry farmers expect the strawberry price to rise
(E) researchers develop more efficient strawberry harvesting tools

313. If the price of a television set increases by 10 percent and the quantity demanded for television sets decreases by 50 percent,

(A) elasticity is 5 and television set demand is price elastic
(B) elasticity is 0.2 and television set demand is price inelastic
(C) elasticity is 50 and television set demand is elastic
(D) elasticity is 10 and television set demand is elastic
(E) elasticity is 0.02 and television set demand is price inelastic

314. A movie star puts on a particular sunscreen at the beach, and that brand of sunscreen becomes much more popular. This will NOT increase

(A) the market price of that sunscreen
(B) quantity supplied for that sunscreen
(C) supply for that sunscreen
(D) demand for that sunscreen
(E) quantity demanded for that sunscreen

315. A hurricane destroys the alfalfa crop in a coastal region. This will NOT reduce

(A) demand for alfalfa
(B) supply for alfalfa
(C) quantity supplied for alfalfa
(D) quantity demanded for alfalfa
(E) demand for alfalfa substitutes

316. Avocado trees are damaged by hot weather, reducing avocado supply. At the same time, avocados become more popular as a taco ingredient. As a result,

(A) the market price of avocados will increase
(B) the market price of avocados will decrease
(C) equilibrium quantity for avocados will increase
(D) equilibrium quantity for avocados will decrease
(E) the market price of avocados will not change

317. A new diet makes bananas more popular with consumers. A new type of fertilizer makes banana trees more productive. As a result,

(A) the market price of bananas will increase
(B) the market price of bananas will decrease
(C) equilibrium quantity for bananas will increase
(D) equilibrium quantity for bananas will decrease
(E) equilibrium quantity for bananas will not change

318. If the price of a used car increases by 40 percent and the quantity demanded for used cars decreases by 10 percent,

(A) elasticity is 0.25 and used car demand is price inelastic
(B) elasticity is 4 and used car demand is price elastic
(C) elasticity is 0.4 and used car demand is price inelastic
(D) elasticity is 2.5 and used car demand is price elastic
(E) used car demand is neither price inelastic nor elastic

319. Which regulation could result in a dead weight loss?

(A) price supports for agricultural goods
(B) a minimum wage law
(C) a rent control law
(D) a maximum interest rate on payday loans
(E) all of the above

320. When the market equilibrium price and the market equilibrium quantity are located at the same point,

(A) oversupply exists
(B) undersupply exists
(C) a dead weight loss is not present
(D) an effective price floor is present
(E) an effective price ceiling is present

321. A consumer buys three apples. Which purchase prices would reflect the law of diminishing marginal utility?

(A) $1 for the first apple, $2 for the second apple, and $3 for the third apple
(B) $2 for each apple
(C) $3 for the first apple, $2 for the second apple, and $3 for the third apple
(D) $3 for the first apple, $2 for the second apple, and $1 for the third apple
(E) $6 for all three apples

322. Which type of business has multiple owners who are each liable for the business?

(A) corporation
(B) sole proprietorship
(C) partnership
(D) horizontally integrated business
(E) vertically integrated business

323. If a business has hundreds of owners who are protected by limited liability, it is a(n)

(A) partnership
(B) sole proprietorship
(C) corporation
(D) monopoly
(E) oligopoly

324. Suppose an ice cream producer buys a competing ice cream producer. This is an example of

(A) vertical integration
(B) horizontal integration
(C) a monopoly
(D) an oligopoly
(E) a corporation

325. Spillover costs are also known as

(A) negative externalities
(B) positive externalities
(C) principal-agent problem
(D) excessive regulation
(E) price competition

326. Positive externalities include

(A) infrastructure investments
(B) employee training
(C) sales for other businesses in the same area
(D) network effect
(E) all of the above

327. Many small farms are producing oranges. There is little differentiation among the oranges, and farms enter and exit the orange industry on a regular basis. As a result,

(A) the market is not very competitive
(B) the orange farms have low pricing power
(C) the orange farms have high pricing power
(D) the orange farms have established an oligopoly
(E) the orange farms have large economies of scale

328. A tax software firm has 40 percent market share. Its main competitor has 30 percent market share. If the first firm wants to gain market share, it should

(A) invest in software patents to create stronger barriers to entry
(B) consider how the other tax software company will respond to its business decisions
(C) attempt to become a price maker rather than a price taker
(D) reduce prices to attract customers from the other tax software company
(E) buy out the other tax software company

329. Many clothing stores are competing for customers in a city by offering unique styles. These clothing stores are likely to

(A) open for business or shut down infrequently
(B) spend much of their revenue on ads
(C) consider other clothing stores' strategic plans before making business decisions
(D) be unable to raise prices without losing all of their customers
(E) have detailed information about clothing buyers and other clothing stores

330. A water company has 100 percent market share in a city. To make the water market most efficient, the government should

(A) separate the water company into several firms to end its monopoly
(B) eliminate price regulations on water to encourage competition
(C) grant the water company a natural monopoly
(D) allow any firm to build water pipes to homes
(E) shut down the water company for violating antitrust laws

The following graph shows a gas station's demand curve for gasoline. Refer to this graph for questions 331–333.

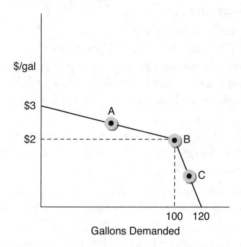

331. Which point on the demand curve would allow the gas station to earn the most revenue?

(A) point A
(B) point B
(C) point C
(D) none of these points
(E) A firm with this demand curve would not be profitable.

332. If the gas station sold gasoline at price point C, what would that indicate?

(A) peak oil
(B) additional gas stations entering the market
(C) an increase in gasoline demand
(D) a price war
(E) non-price competition

333. If the gas station was selling gasoline for $2.50 per gallon,

(A) the gas station would have an inelastic demand curve
(B) the gas station would have an elastic demand curve
(C) competing gas stations would raise prices to $2.50 per gallon
(D) the gas station would maximize revenue
(E) firms would not enter the gasoline market

334. The wholesaler that delivers gas to the gas station decides to raise its prices. If the gas station has a kinked demand curve and the price is at the equilibrium price point,

(A) it will raise its gasoline price by less than the price increase set by the wholesaler

(B) it will raise its gasoline price by more than the price increase set by the wholesaler

(C) it will maintain its gasoline price if the wholesaler's price increase is small, absorbing the cost difference

(D) it will reduce its gasoline price to capture market share

(E) it will maintain its gasoline price even if the price increase is very large

335. A golf club manufacturer has a marginal cost of $50 and marginal revenue of $50 for a golf club. Its average cost for a golf club is $60 and the price at the equilibrium price point is $80. If it sells 100 golf clubs at the equilibrium price point, what is its economic profit?

(A) Its economic profit is $8,000, or equilibrium price × quantity demanded.

(B) Its economic profit is $5,000, or marginal revenue × quantity demanded.

(C) Its economic profit is $2,000, or (equilibrium price – average cost) × quantity demanded.

(D) Its economic profit is $3,000, or (equilibrium price – marginal cost) × quantity demanded.

(E) Its economic profit is $6,000, or marginal cost × quantity demanded.

336. A year later, the golf club manufacturer's average cost is $70 and the equilibrium price point is also $70. This likely happened because

(A) other firms saw the opportunity for an economic profit and began manufacturing golf clubs

(B) consumers lost interest in playing golf

(C) equipment in the golf club factory broke down

(D) raw materials for golf club production became less expensive

(E) golf club manufacturers left the market

337. Two software companies cross-license their patents to one another, giving both firms access to patents held by either company. This is an attempt to create

(A) a monopoly
(B) an economy of scale
(C) a barrier to entry
(D) monopolistic competition
(E) D and C

338. A hydropower plant has a natural monopoly on supplying power to a city and a pharmaceutical company has a monopoly on a patented drug. The difference between these monopolies is

(A) the hydro plant has a temporary monopoly
(B) the pharmaceutical company has a temporary monopoly
(C) the pharmaceutical company has been granted its monopoly by regulators
(D) both firms are violating antitrust laws
(E) the hydro plant has been granted its monopoly by regulators

339. A pharmaceutical firm is currently earning an economic profit on a patented drug. The patent will expire soon. To continue earning an economic profit, the pharmaceutical firm should

(A) invent a new drug
(B) raise the price of its existing drug
(C) lower the price of its existing drug
(D) stop manufacturing the drug immediately
(E) keep the price of the drug the same

340. An auto factory produces cars at an average cost of $10,000 per car. It invests in a larger facility and its average cost rises to $12,000, reducing its economic profit by $2,000 per car. The auto factory's profit decreased because of

(A) lower production efficiency
(B) new market entrants
(C) economies of scale
(D) a decrease in demand for cars
(E) an increase in demand for cars

341. An apple farm is engaged in perfect competition with other apple farms that sell the same cultivar. To earn an economic profit, the apple farm should

(A) raise the price of its apples
(B) reduce the price of its apples to gain market share
(C) sell a unique apple cultivar
(D) produce apples until MC = MR
(E) hire more employees

342. In a market for microwave ovens, the equation for quantity supplied is $P = 10 + 4(Q)$ and the equation for quantity demanded is $P = 80 - 3(Q)$. What is the equilibrium microwave oven price and quantity?

(A) 80, 420
(B) 50, 90
(C) 80, 90
(D) 50, 10
(E) 80, 130

343. In a market for blenders, the equation for quantity supplied is $P = 80 + 6(Q)$ and the equation for quantity demanded is $400 - 10 (Q)$. What is the equilibrium blender price and quantity?

(A) 20, 420
(B) 200, 20
(C) 140, 15
(D) 20, 160
(E) 480, 60

344. Bread becomes less popular with consumers who want wheat-free diets. Meanwhile, a flood damages wheat crops, so less wheat is available for making bread. As a result,

(A) the market price of bread will increase
(B) the market price of bread will decrease
(C) equilibrium quantity for bread will increase
(D) equilibrium quantity for bread will decrease
(E) equilibrium quantity for bread will not change

345. The price of steel, an input for car manufacturing, falls. At the same time, fewer consumers can afford to buy cars because of a weak economy. As a result,

(A) the market price of cars will increase
(B) the market price of cars will decrease
(C) equilibrium quantity for cars will increase
(D) equilibrium quantity for cars will decrease
(E) the market price of cars will not change

346. In a market for vacuum cleaners, the equation for quantity supplied is P = 575 + 8(Q) and the equation for quantity demanded is 920 − 15(Q). What is the equilibrium vacuum cleaner price and quantity, respectively?

(A) 345, 23
(B) 575, 23
(C) 695, 15
(D) 1095, 10
(E) 1200, 8

347. In a market for refrigerators, the equation for quantity supplied is 1,000 + 3(Q) and the equation for quantity demanded is 5,000 − 5(Q). What is the equilibrium refrigerator price and quantity, respectively?

(A) 1,150, 50
(B) 1,150, 4,000
(C) 4,000, 8
(D) 4,000, 400
(E) 400, 4,000

348. The equilibrium price of apples would decrease if the supply and demand curves for apples shifted, respectively, to the

(A) right, left
(B) left, right
(C) left, left
(D) right, right
(E) none of the above

349. The equilibrium quantity of pears would increase if the supply and demand curves for pears shifted, respectively, to the

(A) right, left
(B) left, right
(C) left, left
(D) right, right
(E) none of the above

350. If the government established an effective price floor for grapes,

(A) quantity supplied would be more than quantity demanded
(B) quantity demanded would be more than quantity supplied
(C) quantity supplied would be equal to quantity demanded
(D) quantity supplied would be less than quantity demanded
(E) none of the above

CHAPTER 3

Factor Markets

351. An auto manufacturer can produce one more car if it hires another employee for $20,000. It can also produce one more car if it buys $10,000 worth of machinery. A car sells on the market for $30,000. To increase output, the auto manufacturer should

(A) sell machinery and hire more employees

(B) lay off employees and buy machinery

(C) hire employees until the cost of the next employee equals the cost of buying machinery to produce another car

(D) buy machinery until the cost of buying machinery to produce another car equals the cost of hiring another employee

(E) none of the above

352. Derived demand is illustrated by which of the following?

(A) Consumers desire automobiles to drive, so car companies hire workers for their factories to manufacture automobiles.

(B) An increase in price increases supply, but demand decreases.

(C) The price of wheat increases due to inclement weather for crops.

(D) The salaries of workers increase; thus the price difference is put on to consumers.

(E) A decrease in the demand for shorts will decrease the demand for flip-flops.

353. A taco stand can hire a worker for $100 and produce 10 more tacos. It can hire five workers at $100 per worker and MP will not change. The taco stand can also purchase an oven for $500 and produce 50 more tacos. The taco stand would earn $600 if it sold 50 more tacos. The taco stand should

(A) hire five workers
(B) purchase an oven
(C) either A or B
(D) leave production unchanged
(E) shut down

354. A pretzel stand can make 80 more pretzels if it hires a second employee for $200. Hiring a third employee would increase pretzel output by 60. It can make 160 more pretzels if it buys an oven for $400. A second oven would increase pretzel output by 120. Pretzels sell for $2.50 each. The pretzel stand should

(A) hire one employee
(B) hire two employees
(C) buy an oven
(D) buy two ovens
(E) hire one employee and buy an oven

355. To calculate marginal revenue product,

(A) multiply the marginal product by the marginal cost
(B) multiply the marginal product by the product price
(C) divide the marginal product by the marginal cost
(D) divide the marginal product by the product price
(E) multiply the marginal revenue by the marginal cost

356. John is starting his own business after years of working as a factory worker. In order to maximize his profit, how many workers should he hire?

(A) He should hire until the marginal cost equals marginal revenue.

(B) He should hire until the marginal product equals marginal factor cost.

(C) He should hire until the marginal cost equals marginal factor cost.

(D) He should hire until the marginal revenue product equals marginal factor cost.

(E) He should hire until the marginal revenue product equals marginal cost.

357. A popcorn factory makes popcorn with salt, cooking oil, and corn kernels. Demand for popcorn decreases. As a result,

(A) demand for salt decreases

(B) demand for cooking oil increases

(C) the popcorn factory will hire more workers

(D) demand for corn kernels increases

(E) the popcorn factory will buy more production equipment

358. The MFC of labor rises in country A and falls in country B. As a result,

(A) manufacturers will hire workers in country A and country B

(B) manufacturers will lay off workers in country A and country B

(C) manufacturers will hire workers in country A and lay off workers in country B

(D) manufacturers will lay off workers in country A and hire workers in country B

(E) employment will remain unchanged in both countries

359. Country X creates a new job training program for its citizens. Country Y reduces its spending on job training for its citizens. As a result,

(A) the MRP for labor will fall in country X and country Y

(B) the MRP for labor will rise in country X and fall in country Y

(C) the MRP for labor will rise in country X and country Y

(D) the MRP for labor will rise in country Y and fall in country X

(E) the MRP for labor in country X and country Y will not change

360. A rancher can buy 10 bags of feed for $8 per bag. Buying 11 bags of feed will cost $9 per bag. MFC for the eleventh bag of feed is

(A) $8
(B) $9
(C) $10
(D) $11
(E) $19

361. Demand for raw materials is a

(A) direct demand
(B) positive externality
(C) fixed cost
(D) derived demand
(E) negative externality

Refer to the following graph for questions 362 and 363. Wheat is an input for bread.

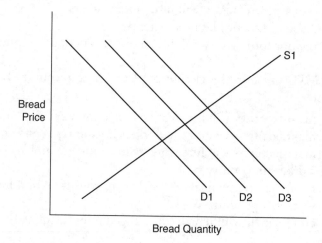

362. If demand for bread shifts from D2 to D3, what happens to the market for wheat?

(A) Demand for wheat rises.
(B) Demand for wheat falls.
(C) Demand for wheat stays the same.
(D) Quantity demanded falls for wheat.
(E) The price of wheat falls.

363. In this example, demand for wheat and bread can be described, respectively, as

(A) derived demand and direct demand
(B) direct demand and derived demand
(C) both are derived demand
(D) both are direct demand
(E) unrelated to one another

364. If more workers moved to towns where automotive plants were located, what will happen to the labor supply curve for auto manufacturers?

(A) The labor supply curve will become horizontal.
(B) The labor supply curve will become vertical.
(C) The labor supply curve will shift to the left.
(D) The labor supply curve will shift to the right.
(E) There would be no change.

365. How would advancements in technology affect a firm's labor demand curve?

(A) It would become horizontal.
(B) It would become vertical.
(C) It would shift to the right.
(D) It would shift to the left.
(E) There would be no change.

366. A lawnmower factory sells lawnmowers for $200. With one worker, it can make three lawnmowers. With two workers, it can make five lawnmowers. With three workers, it can make six lawnmowers. If the MFC for labor decreased from $400 to $200, the lawnmower factory would

(A) hire one worker
(B) hire two workers
(C) leave its workforce unchanged
(D) lay off one worker
(E) lay off two workers

367. A taco truck has no local competitors. With four workers, it can make 100 tacos and sell them for $4 each. With five workers, it can make 150 tacos, but the market price will fall to $3 per taco. The taco truck will hire a fifth worker if the MFC of labor is equal to

(A) $100
(B) $50
(C) $150
(D) $200
(E) $400

368. A cupcake store has no local competitors. With three workers, it can make 100 cupcakes and sell them for $2 each. If it hires a fourth worker, it can make 200 cupcakes and sell them for $1.50 each. MRP for the fourth worker is

(A) $200
(B) $150
(C) $100
(D) $50
(E) $0

369. If a community college canceled its nursing classes, what will happen to the labor supply curve for nearby hospitals?

(A) It will become vertical.
(B) It will become horizontal.
(C) It will shift to the left.
(D) It will shift to the right.
(E) It will not change.

370. A food processing company uses onions to make onion rings. If the price of onions increased, and onions and labor are complementary resources, what would happen to the food processing company's labor demand curve?

(A) It will become vertical.
(B) It will become horizontal.
(C) It will shift to the left.
(D) It will shift to the right.
(E) There would be no change.

371. A motorcycle factory uses machinery and labor to produce motorcycles. If the motorcycle factory purchases more efficient machinery, its demand for labor will decrease if

(A) machinery and labor are complementary resources
(B) machinery and labor are substitute resources
(C) the price of motorcycles rises
(D) demand for motorcycles rises
(E) the price of labor decreases

372. An airplane factory uses machinery and labor to produce airplanes. If the airplane factory buys more efficient machinery, its demand for labor will increase if

(A) the price of airplanes falls
(B) demand for airplanes falls
(C) the price of airplanes increases
(D) machinery and labor are complementary resources
(E) machinery and labor are substitute resources

373. A soda manufacturer produces soda using sugar and carbonated water. If soda has a high elasticity of demand, the soda manufacturer's demand for carbonated water will be

(A) more elastic
(B) less elastic
(C) inelastic
(D) perfectly inelastic
(E) none of the above

374. A restaurant uses wheat tortillas to make tacos. If corn tortillas are available in the market and can be used as a substitute for wheat tortillas, the restaurant's demand for wheat tortillas will be

(A) more elastic
(B) less elastic
(C) inelastic
(D) perfectly inelastic
(E) none of the above

375. A canned soup company uses 10 types of beans to produce minestrone soup and 1 type of bean to produce chili. The firm's demand for a single type of bean used in minestrone soup production, compared to its demand for the chili bean, will be

(A) more elastic
(B) less elastic
(C) just as elastic
(D) inelastic
(E) perfectly inelastic

376. Trucking company A has trucks available for new drivers. Trucking company B does not have any more trucks for new drivers, although new workers can still help unload boxes, which has a smaller impact on productivity than what a new driver would contribute. In comparison with trucking company B, trucking company A's demand for labor will be

(A) more elastic
(B) less elastic
(C) just as elastic
(D) inelastic
(E) perfectly inelastic

377. If firms hire 15 percent fewer production workers when the wage of production workers increases by 45 percent, the price elasticity of labor demand is

(A) 0.33
(B) −0.33
(C) 3
(D) −3
(E) 0

378. If wages rise 40 percent, and 20 percent more production workers enter the market, the price elasticity of labor supply is

(A) 0.5
(B) −0.5
(C) 2
(D) −2
(E) 0

379. If the MFC of labor decreases,

(A) employment increases
(B) unemployment increases
(C) labor demand decreases
(D) labor supply remains unchanged
(E) labor demand remains unchanged

380. Demand for production inputs is a

(A) derived demand
(B) product of positive externalities
(C) product of negative externalities
(D) direct demand
(E) function of the elasticity of demand

381. Consumers demand hamburgers. A restaurant purchases beef to produce hamburgers. Demand for hamburgers is a(n)

(A) derived demand
(B) direct demand
(C) factor of production
(D) cost of production
(E) indirect demand

382. Consumers demand trucks from a truck manufacturer. Because of derived demand, the truck manufacturer will

(A) hire production workers
(B) shut down truck manufacturing plants
(C) create differentiated trucks
(D) offer a discount on last year's truck model
(E) buy radio ads

383. A cookie factory uses wheat and sugar to produce cookies. Wheat and sugar are complementary resources. If the MFC of wheat increases,

(A) sugar demand will fall
(B) sugar demand will rise
(C) sugar demand will stay the same
(D) the price of cookies will fall
(E) the cookie factory will increase production

384. A suit manufacturer has eight employees who can produce 20 suits. The suits sell for $100 each. With nine employees, the firm can produce 24 suits. Marginal revenue product for the ninth employee is

(A) $100
(B) $400
(C) $2,000
(D) $2,400
(E) $800

385. A refrigerator manufacturer has five employees who can produce 10 refrigerators. Each refrigerator sells for $500. With six employees, the firm can produce 12 refrigerators. Marginal revenue product for the sixth employee is

(A) $500
(B) $5,000
(C) $1,000
(D) $6,000
(E) $2,000

386. A saw manufacturer has eight workers who can produce 30 saws. With nine workers, it can produce 25 saws. Each saw sells for $10 on the market. Marginal revenue product for the ninth worker is

(A) $300
(B) $250
(C) $50
(D) –$50
(E) $100

387. A golf club factory has five workers. It pays wages of $500 per day and makes 20 golf clubs, which sell for $50 each. With six workers, it would pay wages of $600 per day and make 24 golf clubs. The golf club factory should hire another worker because

(A) marginal product is positive
(B) marginal revenue product is less than marginal factor cost
(C) marginal product is increasing
(D) total revenue would increase
(E) marginal revenue product is positive

388. A waffle truck sells waffles for $2.50 each. With three employees, its revenue is $250. With four employees, its revenue is $375. Marginal product for the fourth employee is

(A) 50
(B) 150
(C) 100
(D) 250
(E) 200

389. A table manufacturer uses wood to produce tables. Consumers start demanding more tables. Because of derived demand,

(A) the supply of wood will increase
(B) the supply of wood will decrease
(C) the price of wood will increase
(D) the price of wood will decrease
(E) none of the above

390. If employees were required to attend training courses, how would this affect labor productivity?

(A) It would increase.
(B) It would decrease.
(C) It would remain the same.
(D) It would shift the supply curve to the left.
(E) It would have no effect on supply.

391. What is the relationship between the MRP curve and a firm's demand curve?

(A) They both slope downward.
(B) They both slope upward.
(C) There is a diminishing marginal return.
(D) They are horizontal in the long run.
(E) They are vertical in the long run.

392. For an employer, wages are a type of

(A) marginal revenue product
(B) fixed cost
(C) marginal resource cost
(D) marginal product
(E) externality

393. Marginal product is

(A) the total value of all goods produced

(B) the value of goods produced by adding one more production input

(C) the quantity of goods produced by adding one more production input

(D) the total quantity of goods produced

(E) also known as scrap or waste

394. Which of the following would result in higher demand for soda factory workers?

(A) The price of sugar used in soda production increases.

(B) Consumers buy more soda.

(C) Consumers begin drinking tea instead of drinking soda.

(D) Manufacturers shut down soda factories.

(E) Energy drinks gain popularity as an alternative to soda.

395. Which example illustrates derived demand?

(A) A new tomato harvester increases tomato production.

(B) Tomato farm workers go on strike and tomato supply falls.

(C) Ketchup demand increases, and tomato demand increases as a result.

(D) A new pesticide reduces pest damage to the tomato crop.

(E) Scientists discover health benefits of tomatoes.

396. For a manufacturer, the market price of a product, the cost of a labor hour, and the cost of a machine hour are examples of

(A) the determinants of supply

(B) the determinants of demand

(C) the determinants of labor demand

(D) the determinants of elasticity of demand

(E) the determinants of labor supply

397. MRP for a hot dog truck's second, third, and fourth workers is $150, $140, and $130, respectively. The city requires the hot dog truck to pay for health benefits for its workers, increasing MFC for a worker from $130 to $150. The hot dog truck should

(A) hire one more worker
(B) lay off one worker
(C) shut down
(D) lay off two workers
(E) hire two more workers

398. A cabinet manufacturer has seven employees. Each employee earns a wage of $25,000. To attract an eighth employee, it would have to offer a wage of $30,000 to the new employee and current employees would receive a raise to $30,000 as well. MFC for the eighth employee is

(A) $175,000
(B) $65,000
(C) $40,000
(D) $5,000
(E) $240,000

399. A smoothie shop uses bananas to make smoothies. The price of bananas increases. As a result,

(A) MFC increases
(B) profit increases
(C) MP increases
(D) labor demand increases
(E) fixed cost increases

400. If a labor market is a monopsony, in comparison with perfect competition it will have

(A) higher wages
(B) higher unemployment
(C) higher output
(D) less market power
(E) more firms in the market

401. A truck manufacturer can produce one more truck if it hires another employee for $40,000. It can also produce one more truck if it buys $50,000 worth of machinery. A truck sells on the market for $60,000. The truck manufacturer should

(A) hire employees until the cost of the next employee equals the cost of buying machinery to produce another truck

(B) buy machinery until the cost of buying machinery to produce another car equals the cost of hiring another employee

(C) sell machinery and lay off employees

(D) lay off employees and buy machinery

(E) none of the above

402. A single firm that has market power in the labor market is known as a(n)

(A) purely competitive firm

(B) monopsony

(C) oligarchy

(D) monopolistic competition

(E) perfect competition

403. Seth finally realized his dream to open a 24-hour bagel café, which sells wheat bagels. Which of the following scenarios would increase Seth's demand for labor?

(A) The price of wheat increases.

(B) Wheat farmers go on strike.

(C) The price of wheat decreases.

(D) A blight destroys thousands of acres of farmland.

(E) The government establishes a tax on wheat.

404. Derived demand refers to which of the following?

(A) Labor demand for a business is the MRP curve.

(B) Demand for labor comes from the demand for the product produced.

(C) The combination of labor and capital helps minimize total costs.

(D) A business hires workers to the point where MRP = MFC.

(E) Certain firms are wage setters.

405. Wages fall in Arizona and rise in Nevada. As a result,

(A) manufacturers will hire workers in Arizona and Nevada

(B) manufacturers will lay off workers in Arizona and Nevada

(C) manufacturers will hire workers in Arizona and lay off workers in Nevada

(D) manufacturers will lay off workers in Arizona and hire workers in Nevada

(E) employment will remain unchanged in Arizona and Nevada

406. New York offers free university education for state residents, while Nebraska increases tuition for state universities. As a result,

(A) the MRP for labor will rise in New York and Nebraska

(B) the MRP for labor will rise in New York and fall in Nebraska

(C) the MRP for labor will fall in New York and Nebraska

(D) the MRP for labor will fall in New York and rise in Nebraska

(E) the MRP for labor in New York and Nebraska will not change

407. Which of the following is an example of derived demand?

(A) People desire food to eat, so farms invest in tractors and hire workers.

(B) The wages of farmhands increase, so supply decreases and demand increases.

(C) The wages of farmhands decrease, so supply increases and demand decreases.

(D) People desire food to eat, so farms raise the price of food.

(E) none of the above

408. All of the following will increase the demand for doctors EXCEPT

(A) the government requires firms to pay for health care for their employees

(B) all citizens are enrolled in a national health care program

(C) a cure is found for the common cold

(D) flu sweeps across the nation and sickens thousands

(E) venture capitalists invest more money in health care firms

409. If the output effect is greater than the substitution effect, what will happen to the demand for labor?

(A) It increases.
(B) It decreases.
(C) It increases and then gradually decreases.
(D) It decreases and then gradually increases.
(E) It remains the same.

410. An increase in MRP for labor will result in

(A) a decrease in labor demand
(B) an increase in labor demand
(C) a shift of the labor supply curve to the left
(D) no change in labor demand
(E) none of the above

411. The marginal revenue product of labor refers to which of the following?

(A) It measures the cost a business must pay for using one more unit of a factor of production.
(B) It is the value that the next unit of labor brings to the firm.
(C) The combination of labor and capital helps minimize total costs.
(D) A business hires workers to the point where MRP = MRC.
(E) Certain firms are wage setters.

412. If the wage of the last worker hired by a firm is greater than MRP of labor, the firm should

(A) hire more workers
(B) increase supply
(C) decrease supply
(D) lay off workers
(E) do nothing

413. Immigration has which of the following effects?

    (A) It will move the labor supply curve from their country of origin to the right. In the country to which they moved, the curve will shift to the left.

    (B) It will move the labor supply curve from their country of origin to the right. In the country to which they moved, the curve will shift to the right.

    (C) It will move the labor supply curve from their country of origin to the left. In the country to which they moved, the curve will shift to the right.

    (D) It will increase revenue for firms.

    (E) It will decrease the labor demand curves.

414. If the price of raw materials increases, what will happen to labor demand?

    (A) Labor demand will increase.

    (B) Labor demand will remain the same.

    (C) Labor demand will decrease.

    (D) Labor demand will drive prices lower.

    (E) Labor demand will have no effect on price.

415. What will happen to labor demand if the price of a complementary resource rises?

    (A) Labor demand will decrease.

    (B) Labor demand will remain the same.

    (C) Labor demand will increase.

    (D) Labor demand will force the price of the product lower.

    (E) Labor demand will have no effect on price.

416. The least-cost hiring rule refers to

    (A) firms that are wage setters

    (B) a business hiring workers to the point where MRP = MFC

    (C) the combination of labor and capital helping minimize total costs

    (D) measuring the cost a business must pay for using one more unit of a factor of production

    (E) the value that the next unit of a resource brings to the firm

417. How does a monopsony find the equilibrium number of workers to hire?

(A) MRP = MFC
(B) MRP < MFC
(C) MRC > MFC
(D) MC < MB
(E) MC = MB

418. Demand for labor is a

(A) derived demand
(B) product of positive externalities
(C) product of negative externalities
(D) direct demand
(E) function of the elasticity of demand

419. All else equal, as the MFC of labor increases,

(A) unemployment decreases
(B) employment decreases
(C) the supply of labor remains the same
(D) demand remains the same
(E) none of the above

420. Diners wish to eat food at a restaurant. Because of derived demand, the restaurant will

(A) spend money on television ads
(B) buy cooking ingredients
(C) reduce prices because of a decline in rent costs
(D) petition regulators to reduce its taxes
(E) create a differentiated menu

421. An auto parts manufacturer has five workers who can produce 10 auto parts. These parts sell for $3 each. If it hires a sixth worker, it can produce 15 auto parts. Marginal revenue product for the sixth worker is

(A) $45
(B) $30
(C) $5
(D) $15
(E) $50

422. An ice cream stand has eight employees. They can produce 20 ice cream cones, which sell for $2 each. If it hires a ninth employee, it can produce 24 ice cream cones. If it hires a tenth employee, it can produce 27 ice cream cones. Marginal revenue product for the tenth employee is

(A) $40
(B) $48
(C) $8
(D) $6
(E) $54

423. A fishing boat has six crew members, who can catch 40 fish. The fish can be sold at the market for $4 each. If the boat hires a seventh crew member, the total catch will be 35 fish. Marginal revenue product for the seventh crew member is

(A) $160
(B) $140
(C) $20
(D) –$20
(E) $0

424. A hot dog stand has four workers. It pays wages of $400 per day and makes 100 hot dogs, which it sells for $5 each. With five workers, it would pay an additional $120 in wages and make 20 more hot dogs. The hot dog stand should not hire the fifth worker because

(A) marginal product would be negative
(B) total revenue would fall
(C) marginal product is declining
(D) marginal revenue product is less than marginal factor cost
(E) marginal factor cost is rising

425. A golf club manufacturer uses graphite to produce golf clubs. Consumers start demanding more golf clubs. Because of derived demand,

(A) the price of graphite will increase
(B) the price of graphite will decrease
(C) the supply of graphite will increase
(D) the supply of graphite will decrease
(E) none of the above

426. A taco truck sells tacos for $3 each. With four employees, its revenue is $450. If it hires a fifth employee, revenue will be $600. Marginal product for the fifth employee is

(A) 200
(B) 150
(C) 100
(D) 50
(E) 30

427. A surfboard manufacturer adds a seventh worker. Total revenue increases from $900 to $1,000. Production increases from 18 to 20 surfboards. Marginal revenue for a surfboard is

(A) $100
(B) $50
(C) $45
(D) $55
(E) $20

428. Marginal revenue is equal to

(A) the market price of the next unit of output
(B) the cost of the next unit of output
(C) market price multiplied by marginal production
(D) marginal production divided by market price
(E) the average price of a unit of output

429. Marginal resource cost is equal to

(A) marginal revenue multiplied by the cost of a unit of output
(B) total cost for producing every unit of output
(C) the cost of producing the next unit of output
(D) the average cost of producing a unit of output
(E) total revenue divided by the market price of a unit of output

430. Which of the following would NOT result in higher demand for car factory workers?

(A) The cost of steel used in car manufacturing decreases.
(B) Consumers purchase more cars.
(C) Consumers begin taking the train to work instead of driving their cars.
(D) Firms construct more car manufacturing plants.
(E) Bus ridership declines as a result of economic expansion.

431. Which example illustrates derived demand?

(A) Consumers increase their purchases of corn tortillas, so the price of corn rises.

(B) Technology makes wheat production more efficient so the output of wheat flour increases.

(C) Workers move from country A to country B in search of economic opportunities.

(D) A truck factory shuts down after workers go on strike.

(E) A heat wave causes the sugar beet price to rise on the market.

432. MRP for a hot dog stand's fifth, sixth, and seventh workers is $140, $120, and $100, respectively. If the wage for a hot dog stand worker is $120, the hot dog stand should

(A) employ four workers

(B) employ five workers

(C) employ six workers

(D) employ seven workers

(E) employ eight workers

433. MRP for a shaved ice stand's first, second, and third workers is $95, $90, and $85 per day, respectively. The shaved ice stand hires workers until MRP = MFC. The government increases the minimum daily wage from $85 to $90. The shaved ice stand should

(A) hire one more worker

(B) lay off one worker

(C) shut down

(D) lay off two workers

(E) hire two more workers

434. A skateboard manufacturer is the only employer in a small town. It has 10 workers who each earn $40,000. It can hire another worker at a wage of $50,000 and produce skateboards worth $60,000. This would make its current workers demand a wage of $50,000 as well. If the firm hired another worker,

(A) profit would increase because MFC < MRP

(B) profit would be unchanged because MFC = MRP

(C) profit would fall because MFC > MRP

(D) profit would increase because the skateboard manufacturer has a monopoly

(E) none of the above

435. An auto body shop has six employees, who each earn $30,000. If it hired a seventh employee, it would have to pay all of its employees $40,000 each. MFC for the seventh employee is

(A) $10,000
(B) $30,000
(C) $40,000
(D) $100,000
(E) $280,000

436. A soft drink factory can buy 10 tons of sugar for $200 per ton. If it buys 11 tons of sugar, it must pay $250 per ton. MFC for the eleventh ton of sugar is

(A) $200
(B) $250
(C) $500
(D) $550
(E) $750

437. A sandwich shop uses roast beef to make sandwiches. The price of roast beef decreases. As a result,

(A) MFC decreases
(B) profit decreases
(C) MP decreases
(D) labor demand decreases
(E) fixed cost decreases

438. If a labor market is an oligopsony, in comparison with perfect competition it will have

(A) lower wages
(B) lower unemployment
(C) higher output
(D) less market power
(E) more firms in the market

439. A bicycle manufacturer purchases aluminum to make bicycles. Demand for aluminum is a

(A) negative externality
(B) fixed cost
(C) derived demand
(D) negative externality
(E) factor of production

440. A cupcake manufacturer uses frosting to make cupcakes. If demand for cupcakes increases,

(A) frosting demand will shift to the right
(B) frosting demand will shift to the left
(C) frosting demand will not change
(D) frosting price will decrease
(E) frosting quantity will decrease

CHAPTER 4

Market Failure and the Role of Government

441. Christopher recently moved out of his parents' house and purchased his own house. He worked all summer on the front and backyard lawns and gardens to make his new house look nice. Christopher's new neighbors all appreciated the hard work he put into the outside of his house, as it helped beautify their block and neighborhood. The results of Christopher's efforts are known as

(A) the free-rider problem
(B) a market failure
(C) the spillover effect
(D) the Gini ratio
(E) negative externalities

442. A good that is excludable to other consumers and rivals is known as a

(A) public good
(B) quasi-public good
(C) positive externality
(D) common resource
(E) private good

443. If a positive externality emerges, in regard to the demand curve

(A) MEB is not represented
(B) MEC is represented
(C) MSC is represented
(D) marginal private benefits are not represented
(E) none of the above

444. If the U.S. government increases a tax to help redistribute income from the wealthy to the poor, it is following a

(A) proportional tax system
(B) tariff system
(C) progressive tax system
(D) regressive tax system
(E) neutral tax system

445. A negative externality will exist when

(A) all consumers receive an equal share of economic resources
(B) spillover costs are given to others not directly involved in the consumption or production of a good or service
(C) the production of a good or service creates a spillover benefit
(D) members of a community pay for a good or service while others do not yet benefit
(E) there is a large unequal distribution of income in a society

446. The private sector will NOT provide for a public good or service due to

(A) the income effect
(B) the interest rates effect
(C) the free-rider problem
(D) spillover costs
(E) all of the above

447. A positive externality will exist when

(A) all consumers receive an equal share of economic resources
(B) spillover costs are given to others not directly involved in the consumption or production of a good or service
(C) the production of a good or service creates a spillover benefit
(D) members of a community pay for a good or service while others do not yet benefit
(E) there is an equal distribution of income in a society

448. If firms overproduce a good or service and charge a price that is too low, it is likely that

(A) a negative externality exists
(B) a positive externality exists
(C) spillover costs are subsidized by the government
(D) the firm is at the shutdown point
(E) A, C, and D

449. Regulation and antitrust laws

(A) are some of the economic functions of the government that help encourage competition
(B) are some of the economic functions of the government that dissuade competition
(C) are effective only in a market economy
(D) assist the government to redistribute income and wealth
(E) are methods used by the government to promote positive externalities

The following graph represents a government intervention in response to a market that produced a positive externality. Use the information provided in the graph to answer questions 450 and 451.

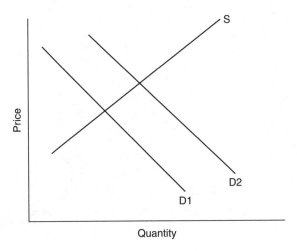

450. How may the government intervene to move the demand curve from D1 to D2?

(A) Give a subsidy to buyers.
(B) Tax buyers.
(C) Influence the business making the good to stop production.
(D) Increase the money supply.
(E) Decrease the money supply.

451. If the government intervenes and demand moves to D2, all of the following are true EXCEPT

(A) resources are being efficiently used
(B) MEB is now represented in the demand curve
(C) output is now at the socially optimum level
(D) MEB is not represented in the demand curve
(E) buyers may be receiving a subsidy

The following graph represents a government intervention in response to a market that produced a negative externality. Use the information provided in the graph to answer questions 452 and 453.

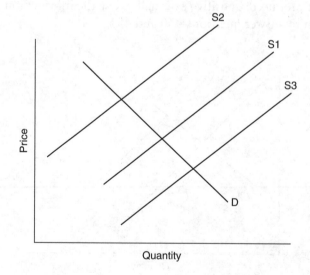

452. If the government imposes restrictions on producers, this could

(A) shift the supply curve from S1 to S2

(B) shift the supply curve from S2 to S3

(C) have no effect on the supply curve

(D) create a new demand curve

(E) both A and D

453. If the supply curve is shifted to S2, which of the following is TRUE?

(A) Marginal social costs are not reflected in the supply curve.

(B) Marginal social costs are reflected in the supply curve.

(C) Output has reached the socially optimum level.

(D) The demand curve will also shift to the left.

(E) both B and C

454. A private business will NOT produce a good like a public radio station because

(A) MC is greater than MB

(B) there is zero profit for this good

(C) the government owns a monopoly for this type of service

(D) the free-rider problem exists

(E) all of the above

455. The idea that taxes and a person's income should vary directly is known as

(A) the marginal propensity to consume

(B) the marginal propensity to save

(C) the free-rider problem

(D) the ability to pay principle of taxation

(E) marginal cost

456. The reason a general sales tax is regressive is because

(A) low-income families pay a higher portion of their income than high-income families do

(B) the tax is paid for by the seller, not the buyer

(C) the tax is paid for by the buyer, not the seller

(D) low-income families pay less of the tax than households with higher incomes do

(E) tax rates do not vary as compared to income

457. The fact that a firefighter's job is more dangerous than a college professor's job is an example of

(A) compensating differential
(B) a negative externality
(C) the free-rider problem
(D) the ability to pay principle
(E) the benefits received principle

458. Of the following, which is a public good?

(A) a limousine
(B) tickets to a baseball game
(C) a subscription to the *New York Times*
(D) a fighter jet
(E) a bowl of ice cream

459. A "flat tax" is also known as

(A) ability to pay tax
(B) benefits received tax
(C) proportional tax
(D) income tax
(E) property tax

460. Industrialized nations often produce negative externalities in the form of pollution. What is a possible solution to fix this negative externality?

(A) a per-unit tax on consumers
(B) a government subsidy for consumers
(C) a government subsidy for producers
(D) a per-unit tax on producers
(E) a flat tax on both producers and consumers

461. Last year Anna earned $50,000 in gross income and paid $10,000 in taxes. She recently received a promotion. So next year she will earn $75,000 in gross income and pay $15,000 in taxes. This increase in taxes is a result of

(A) a regressive tax
(B) a progressive tax
(C) a proportional tax
(D) an ability to pay tax
(E) none of the above

462. Fire protection provided by a fire department is an example of a(n)

(A) private good
(B) inferior good
(C) normal good
(D) public good
(E) complementary good

463. Nation A has a higher Gini ratio than nation B. You can conclude that nation A

(A) has a highly unequal distribution of income compared to nation B
(B) has a more equal distribution of income compared to nation B
(C) has an equal distribution of income compared to nation B
(D) is allocating its resources to full efficiency
(E) is at full employment with no inflation

Use the following graph to answer questions 464 and 465.

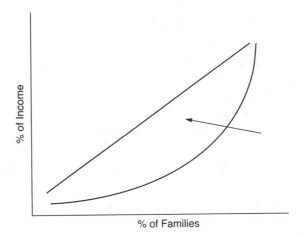

464. The graph represents

(A) the percentage of income tax families pay in the United States
(B) the percentage of families paying a regressive tax on their incomes
(C) the percentage of families paying a flat tax on their incomes
(D) the percentage of families paying a progressive tax in the United States
(E) the distribution of income among families in the United States

465. The arrow in the graph is pointing to the area between a perfect distribution of income and the actual distribution of income. If the Gini ratio is 0.9, it is said that this graph represents

(A) a highly unequal distribution of income
(B) a very equal distribution of income
(C) most families having the same socioeconomic status
(D) a society benefiting from egalitarianism
(E) a negative externality

466. Suppose Anna earns $50,000 a year and pays $10,000 in taxes. Her friend Sarah earns $100,000 a year and pays only $12,000 a year in taxes. This is an example of

(A) a progressive tax
(B) a proportional tax
(C) a negative externality
(D) being in a higher tax bracket
(E) a regressive tax

467. Market power, a person's ability, human capital, and discrimination are all factors that may result in

(A) an unequal distribution of wealth
(B) negative externalities
(C) positive externalities
(D) a low Gini ratio
(E) a fair and equal distribution of wealth

468. If income increases and the marginal tax rate falls, this is also known as a

(A) regressive tax
(B) proportional tax
(C) flat tax
(D) progressive tax
(E) tax bracket

469. As income increases, the marginal tax rate increases. This is known as a

(A) progressive tax
(B) regressive tax
(C) flat tax
(D) proportional tax
(E) tax bracket

470. A ride in a taxicab is a form of

(A) a public good
(B) a private good
(C) a government subsidy
(D) a positive externality
(E) the free-rider problem

471. NASA, an organization run by the federal government, sends a satellite into space. The satellite broadcasts information about the solar system to people around the world at no charge. The satellite represents

(A) a private good
(B) a government subsidy
(C) a positive externality
(D) a public good
(E) the free-rider problem

472. The government helps with the redistribution of income

(A) only in a command economy
(B) only in a mixed economy
(C) through taxes
(D) through proportional taxes only
(E) only in a market economy

473. A Pigovian tax will result in

(A) MPC = P
(B) MPC < P
(C) MSC = P
(D) MSC > P
(E) MSC < P

474. A Pigovian subsidy will result in

(A) MPB = S
(B) MPB < S
(C) MSB < S
(D) MSB = S
(E) MSB > S

475. A Pigovian tax could be

(A) a flat tax on personal income
(B) a property tax applied to all homeowners
(C) a sales tax applied to all goods
(D) a vice tax on sugary soft drinks
(E) a flat tax on capital gains

476. A Pigovian subsidy could be

(A) a standard deduction available to all consumers
(B) a lower tax rate for all consumer goods
(C) a subsidy for electric vehicles
(D) a lower tariff rate for all imported products
(E) a tax refund sent to all consumers

477. A shopkeeper earns $100,000 and pays $15,000 in pension taxes. The next year, the shopkeeper earns $150,000 and pays $15,000 in pension taxes. The pension tax is

(A) progressive
(B) based on ability to pay
(C) proportional
(D) regressive
(E) none of the above

478. Five gas stations sell 100,000 barrels of fuel. Economists calculate that burning this fuel results in air pollution that costs society $1,000,000. If regulators want the marginal social cost of fuel to equal the marginal social benefit of fuel, they should

(A) pay a $10/barrel subsidy to gas stations
(B) levy a $10/barrel tax on gas stations
(C) make each gas station pay $200,000 in taxes
(D) shut down the gas stations
(E) none of the above

479. The government decides to encourage bus travel by paying a subsidy to bus companies for each mile traveled. As a result of the subsidy,

(A) bus supply will shift to the right
(B) bus demand will shift to the right
(C) bus supply will shift to the left
(D) bus demand will shift to the left
(E) none of the above

480. The government encourages consumers to buy efficient refrigerators by paying a rebate to consumers. As a result of the rebate,

(A) demand for efficient refrigerators will shift to the right
(B) supply for efficient refrigerators will shift to the right
(C) demand for efficient refrigerators will shift to the left
(D) supply for efficient refrigerators will shift to the left
(E) none of the above

481. Which item is a public good?

(A) transport provided by a personal automobile
(B) law enforcement provided by a police car
(C) delivery provided by a pizza delivery car
(D) transport provided by a rental car
(E) transport provided by a personal truck

482. Country X had a Gini ratio of 0.40 last year. This year, country X reported that its Gini ratio decreased to 0.35. We can conclude that

(A) the income distribution in country X has become more equal
(B) the income distribution in country X has become less equal
(C) country X is experiencing a recession
(D) country X is experiencing an economic expansion
(E) country X has improved its freedom of the press

483. Country Y had a Gini ratio of 0.25 last year. This year, its Gini ratio was 0.30. This indicates that

(A) the income distribution in country Y has become more equal
(B) the income distribution in country Y has become less equal
(C) country Y is experiencing a recession
(D) country Y is experiencing an economic expansion
(E) country Y reduced its business regulations

484. Country A has a Gini ratio of 0.20. Country B has a Gini ratio of 0.25. Country C has a Gini ratio of 0.30. This indicates that

(A) country C has a more equal income distribution than country B
(B) country B has a more equal income distribution than country A
(C) country C has a more equal income distribution than country A
(D) country B has a more equal income distribution than country C
(E) none of the above

485. Countries D and E have the same Gini ratio. Country D implements a proportional tax and country E implements a progressive tax. As a result,

(A) country E will have a higher Gini ratio than country D
(B) country D will have a higher Gini ratio than country E
(C) country D will still have the same Gini Ratio as country E
(D) country D will have the same Gini ratio as country E
(E) none of the above

486. Cities B and C have the same Gini ratio. City B implements a flat tax and city C implements a regressive tax. As a result,

(A) city B will have a higher Gini ratio than city C
(B) city C will have a higher Gini ratio than city B
(C) city C will still have the same Gini Ratio as city B
(D) both cities will have the same Gini ratio
(E) none of the above

487. The government allows all citizens to hunt birds on federal land. The birds are an example of a

(A) public good
(B) common resource
(C) quasi-public good
(D) private good
(E) none of the above

488. A city charges drivers a toll to cross a bridge. The bridge has enough capacity to handle normal traffic. The bridge is a

(A) common resource
(B) public good
(C) quasi-public good
(D) private good
(E) none of the above

489. A freeway is open to all citizens and does not charge a toll. At rush hour, the freeway does not have enough room for all drivers. During rush hour, the freeway is

(A) a public good
(B) a private good
(C) a quasi-public good
(D) a common resource
(E) none of the above

490. According to the Coase theorem, consumers can reach an agreement when

(A) negotiating costs are low
(B) marginal cost does not equal marginal benefit
(C) the government intervenes
(D) positive externalities are present
(E) negative externalities are not present

491. The Coase theorem would not apply to a factory that was polluting a river near a city because

(A) the pollution affects many people
(B) the factory's liabilities are very clear
(C) negotiating costs are low
(D) the negotiation process is efficient
(E) there are no negative externalities

492. If firms underproduce a good or service and charge a price that is too high, it is likely

(A) a negative externality exists
(B) a positive externality exists
(C) spillover costs are high
(D) the economy is expanding
(E) there is a government subsidy

493. When a government subsidizes student grants to attend university for all students,

    (A) it is creating a consumer subsidy

    (B) it is creating a producer subsidy

    (C) university education is a public good

    (D) university education is a common resource

    (E) both A and D

494. When a government grants a property tax exemption to universities, but many students still cannot afford to attend universities,

    (A) it is creating a consumer subsidy

    (B) it is creating a producer subsidy

    (C) university education is a public good

    (D) university education is a private good

    (E) both B and D

495. The government provides elementary school education to all students, and once the students graduate they begin work at local businesses. Productivity increases at these businesses. This is an example of

    (A) spillover costs

    (B) spillover benefits

    (C) negative externalities

    (D) the Gini ratio

    (E) market failure

496. Phantom demand refers to

    (A) goods and services that consumers purchased in the past

    (B) unaffordable goods and services

    (C) market failure

    (D) demand for public goods that consumers cannot purchase directly

    (E) demand that would exist if the economy expanded

497. The demand curve for a public good is

    (A) the horizontal sum of each consumer's demand curve

    (B) the vertical sum of each consumer's demand curve

    (C) not measurable

    (D) always horizontal

    (E) always vertical

Use the following graph to answer questions 498 and 499.

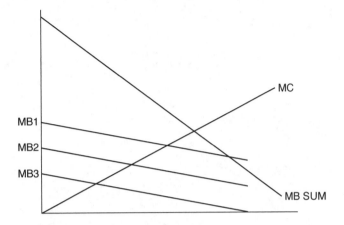

498. The graph shows demand curves for a(n)

(A) private good
(B) inferior good
(C) luxury good
(D) public good
(E) capital good

499. The equilibrium price of this public good will be

(A) MB1 = MC
(B) MB2 = MC
(C) MB3 = MC
(D) MB SUM = MC
(E) none of the above

500. In comparison to the demand curve for all consumers, the slope of the demand curve for an individual consumer of a public good will be

(A) more steep
(B) more flat
(C) the same
(D) horizontal
(E) vertical

ANSWERS

Chapter 1

1. (C) Choice (C) is the best answer because the resources in the world are limited, yet our desires and wants are unlimited. The study of economics attempts to examine the ways these unlimited wants and desires may be satisfied.

2. (D) Choice (D) is the correct answer because Deirdre can make only one decision regarding how she will spend her time. An opportunity cost represents the next best thing missed out on. In this case, it is missing out on the $10/hour babysitting job and not the $7/hour library job. All other choices are incorrect because they incorporate the two choices, whereas opportunity costs represent only the next best alternative.

3. (A) Choice (A) is the correct answer because with any choice people make, they must look at the relationship between marginal benefit and marginal cost. If a decision, whether it be purchasing an item or going for a walk, costs more than the benefit, then the person should not do it.

4. (E) Choice (E) is the correct answer because factors of production refer to the inputs actually used to manufacture the product, while money is used to purchase these inputs.

5. (A) Choice (A) is correct because the production possibilities curve represents the maximum output between two goods using scarce resources. As such, it represents the increasing opportunity costs incurred when the production shifts to more of one product than the other. The more a producer chooses to make of a product, the more the opportunity cost increases for the product not being produced. This represents the law of increasing costs.

6. (E) The correct choice is (E) because trade will exist between two countries if there is a comparative advantage between the two countries, or each country is producing its good at a lower opportunity cost than the other.

7. (D) The correct choice is (D) because if a society is overallocating, then it is not utilizing its resources to allocative efficiency. This would imply that the marginal benefit (MB) for producing goods and services with these resources is less than the marginal cost (MC). In any economic decision, it is best to have either MB > MC or MB = MC.

8. (C) Choice (C) is the best answer because it best reflects the idea of comparative advantage. If a producer can make a good at a lower opportunity cost than all other producers, it is said that he or she has a comparative advantage. Richard can mow the lawn at a lower opportunity cost than Michele, so it would be mutually beneficial if he mowed the lawn and Michele walked the dog.

9. (C) A command economy is the opposite of a free market (where prices and the answers to the fundamental questions of economics are answered by consumers and producers). A command economy is also known as a planned economy.

10. (A) The production possibilities curve represents the maximum production capabilities of two goods based on an economy's available resources. An outward, or rightward, shift of the production possibilities curve represents economic growth. Choice (A) is the best answer because educational training would be an increase in human capital and in production. All the other choices would cause the production possibilities curve to shift to the left.

11. (C) The production possibilities curve represents the maximum output between two goods using scarce resources. Any point lying on the curve would represent the most attainable, productively efficient use of resources. Choice (C) is the correct answer.

12. (E) Choice (E) is correct because the number of resources in the world is limited, yet our desires and wants are unlimited. For example, there is only a finite amount of fossil fuels available on Earth.

13. (B) Choice (B) is the correct answer because opportunity cost refers to the value of what is given up. In this scenario, Joe decided to maximize hot dog production, giving up the opportunity to produce 400 hamburgers with his supplies. The prices of hot dogs and hamburgers are not needed for this calculation.

14. (A) Choice (A) is correct because factors of production refer to all the units that are used in the production of goods and services in hopes of making a profit. They are categorized as land, labor, capital, and entrepreneurship.

15. (B) Choice (B) is correct because the law of increasing costs refers to how the more a good or service is produced, the more its opportunity costs increase. If there is an increase in the production of good A, then the opportunity cost, the next most valuable alternative, increases for good B.

16. (A) Choice (A) is correct because the production possibilities curve is a straight line. This means that where resource materials are best suited for the production of both goods, either opportunity costs are constant or resources are not specialized.

17. (A) Choice (A) is correct because trade will exist between two countries if there is a comparative advantage between the two countries, or each country is producing its good at a lower opportunity cost than the other.

18. (B) Choice (B) is correct because specialization refers to the production of goods based on comparative advantage. If a nation can produce a good at a lower opportunity cost, then it would be beneficial if it specialized in producing that good and traded with another nation that specialized in producing other goods. Consuming more than the production possibilities curve dictates necessitates specialization.

19. (A) Choice (A) is correct. According to the law of comparative advantage, two nations should specialize production by producing goods at the lowest possible cost. These nations should then engage in trade for the products they stopped producing to specialize. Since Spain has a lower opportunity cost for producing soccer balls as compared to Germany, it should stop producing golf balls and focus on soccer balls.

20. (A) Choice (A) is the best answer because a free market guides producers to the three fundamental questions: What to produce? How to produce? For whom to produce? All businesses must decide what to produce based on limited resources (scarcity). Entrepreneurs must answer the question "How to produce?" because it affects major business decisions. Should the product be produced domestically or abroad? Should outside contractors be consulted? In a free market, the question of for whom to produce is dictated by demand.

21. (D) Choice (D) is correct because economic growth occurs if any of the factors of production increase. Any choice that refers to a decrease in the factors of production may be eliminated. Choice (B) is incorrect because although a division of labor is highly efficient, it is ambiguous if it would create economic growth. A diseconomy of scale refers to an increase in cost when output is increased.

22. (B) Choice (B) is correct because with any choice people make, they must look at the relationship between marginal benefit and marginal cost. If a decision, whether it be purchasing an item or going for a walk, costs more than the benefit, then the person should not do it.

23. (C) Choice (C) is correct because opportunity cost is what is given up when someone makes a decision. If your school decides to construct a new performing arts center, all of the resources that could have been used in another project are given up. The resources must go into the construction of the performing arts center.

24. (E) Choice (E) is correct because allocative efficiency refers to the measure of the benefit or utility gained from the use of material resources. If resources are being used efficiently, then the production possibilities curve will remain the same and production will lie on the line, not inside. All other choices would result in a shift of the production possibilities curve because these would be changes in the factors of production.

25. (D) Choice (D) is the best answer because marginal analysis refers to the decision-making process based on marginal benefits versus marginal costs.

26. (B) Choice (B) is the best answer because a market system has complete decentralization of decision making for firms and consumers. A mixed economy refers to a combination of capitalism and socialism, where there are elements of centralized planning and a free market. Economies with market systems do not currently exist because every nation's government makes some economic decisions. A command economy is the opposite of a free market (where prices and the answers to the fundamental questions of economics are answered by consumers and producers). A command economy is also known as a planned economy.

27. (C) The best answer is Choice (C). When comparing command economies, mixed economies, or a market economy, the most fundamental differences exist in how these societies answer the three fundamental questions of economics: What to produce? How to produce? For whom to produce?

28. (D) Choice (D) is correct. This refers to the three fundamental questions of economics: What to produce? How to produce? For whom to produce? These questions exist because resources are scarce and people's wants and desires are unlimited.

29. (C) Choice (C) is the best answer. At the point on the production possibilities curve where MB = MC, production is both productively efficient and allocatively efficient.

30. (D) Choice (D) is correct because a market system is characterized by a decentralization of decision making for firms and consumers.

31. (A) Choice (A) is correct because this point is located inside the current production curve, not along the curve. The curve would have to move left to reach this point, shrinking inward. This would indicate fewer resources and less production capacity available, which could indicate a recession.

32. (D) The correct choice is (D) because point E and point D are both on the same production possibilities curve, so resource availability and production capacity have not changed and there is no evidence of recession or economic expansion.

33. (D) The correct choice is (D). If Choice (C) occurred, production would not change, and all other outcomes would shift the curve to the right.

34. (C) The correct answer is (C). The Law of Variable Proportions explains that when a manufacturing process has several inputs, changing a single input affects total production. A restaurant with an understaffed kitchen can benefit from adding food prep workers. Eventually, each food prep worker makes a smaller contribution toward preparing additional meals. If the company hires too many kitchen workers, meal production declines as the workers get in each other's way. The restaurant should stop hiring workers when the cost of hiring an additional food prep worker equals the value of the additional food produced. In other words, the restaurant should stop hiring when marginal cost equals marginal benefit.

35. (C) The correct answer is (C). A nation with a mixed economy often lets the free market handle decisions for most industries and uses a command approach for selected industries, such as industries related to food production or national security. Most nations have mixed economies; a completely free market economy would have no public sector, and a completely command economy would have no private sector.

36. (D) The correct answer is (D). A ruby is not necessary for survival while people need water to remain alive, yet a ruby is much more expensive than a bottle of water. This is the paradox of value. It occurs because rubies are scarcer than bottles of water, and scarcity results in a higher price.

37. (B) The correct answer is (B), the truck. A truck can be driven regularly for more than three years, while the other items will wear out or be used up in less than three years so they are considered nondurable goods.

38. (C) The correct choice is (C), a barter economy. This type of economy preceded the market economy and is very rare now. Barter economies can still exist under special conditions, such as when buyers and sellers wish to evade high taxes or a nation's currency is experiencing hyperinflation.

39. (B) The best choice is (B). The tire factory reaches the profit-maximizing quantity of output when the marginal benefit from hiring a worker to produce tires equals the additional revenue from selling the tires. The tire factory should continue hiring workers if MB > MC and should not hire a worker if MB < MC. Choice (D) would actually cost the company $30,000 per year.

40. (C) The best choice is (C). Marginal utility declines as additional units of a good are purchased. After buying three cans of soda, the consumer considers the fourth can less valuable.

41. (B) The best choice is (B). The law of comparative advantage indicates that France should specialize in producing cheese and Switzerland should specialize in producing chocolate and both countries should trade with one another. If a trade embargo stops this exchange, France would need to produce its own chocolate and Switzerland would need to produce its own cheese. As a result, France would produce less cheese and Switzerland would produce less chocolate.

42. (B) The correct choice is (B). A typical production possibility curve is concave, indicating increasing opportunity costs. As the nation moves toward maximizing production of one crop, its production of the other crop falls more rapidly. That isn't the case here. This lack of increasing opportunity costs indicates that the nation's resources are equally suitable for producing either crop.

43. (E) Choice (E) is the best choice. Specialization creates a concave shape for the production possibilities curve. Specialization can also increase total production by making workers and factories more efficient. An unspecialized economy probably isn't as productive in overall terms as a specialized economy.

44. (D) Choice (D) is correct. The bakery can produce either 300 cookies and 140 loaves of bread at point A, or zero cookies and 160 loaves of bread at point B. Cookie production fell from 300 units to zero, so 300 cookies is the opportunity cost.

45. (C) Choice (C) is correct. At point A the bakery produces 140 loaves of bread, and at point D the bakery produces 80 loaves of bread. Bread production fell by 60 loaves. Cookie production remained unchanged at 300 cookies.

46. (D) Choice (D) is the best answer. A biased technology improves production efficiency for only one good. Choice (A) is incorrect because an economic expansion would increase the maximum production quantity for cars as well.

47. (E) Choice (E) is the best answer. If resources allocated to bread and car production do not change, car quantity will remain the same and bread quantity will increase.

48. (A) Choice (A) is correct. If the spinach quantity doesn't change after the biased technology increases the efficiency of spinach production, the nation must have allocated more resources to lettuce production so the lettuce quantity will increase.

49. (E) Choice (E) is the best answer. Britain gives up less rye to produce cattle and France gives up less cattle to produce rye.

50. (B) Choice (B) is the best answer. Allocatively efficient production occurs at the point on the production possibilities curve where MB = MC.

Chapter 2

51. (A) According to the law of demand, all else being equal, when the price of a good or service increases, the quantity demanded decreases. Choice (A) is the best answer because it is the inverse of the question being asked.

52. (B) Choice (B) is correct because a normal good is a good that increases in demand as income increases. Since Michael received an increase in his yearly salary, there was an increase in demand for steak, and steak is an expensive meat product, it is a normal good. Choice (A) is incorrect because an inferior good is a good for which demand decreases as income increases. Choice (E) is incorrect because eating steak is not a necessity. Choices (C) and (D) are incorrect because eating steak does not affect the determinants of supply and demand.

53. (D) Choice (D) is correct. An inferior good is a good for which demand decreases as income increases. Since Peter received an increase in salary, he can afford better shoes than thrift-store-bought shoes.

54. (E) Choice (E) is correct. Tin is a factor of production used in the production of guitar strings. Firms will produce more guitar strings if the costs related to the production of the product decrease. If the price of tin decreases, then producers are willing and able to produce more due to a decrease in a factor of production.

55. (C) Choice (C) is correct. Remember that people will buy more of a good if the price is low and less of a good if the price is high. This illustrates an inverse relationship. According to the law of demand and all else being equal, when the price of a good or service increases, the quantity demanded decreases.

56. (B) Choice (B) is correct. The law of supply represents the willingness of producers to produce goods at all price levels. The law of supply shows a direct relationship between price and quantity of goods supplied. Therefore, if the price of a good increases, producers are more willing to produce an increased quantity of goods.

57. (A) Choice (A) is correct. Within a market system, consumers and firms are free to consume and produce what they wish. The three fundamental questions asked in an economy are: What to produce? How to produce? For whom to produce? These questions are answered by the decisions made by consumers and producers, where prices are set through the market forces of supply and demand without any government intervention.

58. (B) The question asks for only the quantity supplied, so any question that refers to price may be eliminated. Choice (B) is the best answer because if the price of a good increases, its substitutes will experience an increase in the quantity demanded.

59. (B) The correct choice is (B) because according to the law of demand, if the price of figs increases consumers will demand fewer figs.

60. (E) Tennis rackets and tennis balls are complementary goods. You cannot use a tennis racket without tennis balls. Therefore, if the price of one good increases or decreases, the price of the complementary good increases or decreases. Choice (E) is the best answer because it illustrates the complementary effect.

61. (A) Choice (A) is correct. Chicken is a normal good. Remember that a normal good is a good that increases in demand as income increases. If the demand curve for chicken shifted to the left, then consumer income would show an overall decrease.

62. (C) The correct choice is (C). When income increases and a consumer stops buying an inexpensive good and begins purchasing a more expensive good, this indicates a switch from an inferior good to a superior good.

63. (C) Choice (C) is correct. If the price of hot dogs increases, then the price of hot dog buns will increase as well.

64. (B) Choice (B) is correct. All else being equal, in a free market system, the price of a good or service is determined at the equilibrium point where supply and demand intersect.

65. (A) Choice (A) is correct. The graph represents the inverse relation stated in the law of demand. The graph represents movement from point B to point A. This illustrates that the quantity demanded decreased due to an increase in price.

66. (C) Choice (C) is correct. If the price of a key ingredient decreases, then the cost of production will decrease. This will lead Doherty Industries to offer more of the product at all possible price levels. This illustrates the law of supply.

67. (E) Choice (E) is correct. The producer would gain more revenue by raising the price for an inelastic good. For example, if the gasoline price increased 20 percent and quantity demanded fell 10 percent, gasoline would be inelastic and the revenue from higher-priced gasoline would outweigh sales lost due to the higher price. If the price increased 20 percent and quantity demanded did not change, the good would be considered perfectly inelastic.

68. (A) Choice (A) is correct. Most necessity goods are price inelastic.

69. (B) The elasticity formula is percent change in quantity divided by percent change in price. If the answer is greater than 1, the good is said to be price sensitive, or elastic. If the answer is less than 1, the good is said not to be price sensitive. Therefore, Choice (B) is the best answer because 40/10 = 4.

70. (D) Refer to question 69. Therefore, Choice (D) is the best answer because 0/30 = 0.

71. (B) Choice (B) is correct. Sally's income decreased and her demand for canned vegetables increased as a result, so canned vegetables are an inferior good.

72. (B) The movement from D1 to D2 represents an increase in demand. Choice (B) is the best answer because a decrease in the price of a substitute good would decrease demand for this product and increase demand for the substitute good.

73. (A) The movement from S1 to S2 represents a decrease in supply. Choice (A) is the best answer because if the price of a key ingredient to the production of the product decreased, then production would increase due to a decrease in the costs of production.

74. (D) A price ceiling refers to the maximum price at which a producer is allowed to sell a good or service. This is usually instituted by law from the government and helps ensure fair business practices. An effective price ceiling is set at a point below the equilibrium price.

75. (A) Choice (A) is the best answer because over a longer period of time, producers have a better chance to adjust to a change in price: hire more workers and build more plants. Over time, elasticity of supply will be greater.

76. (C) Choice (C) is correct. Consumer surplus is measured by calculating the difference between what consumers are willing and able to pay for a good or service and its relative market price. A surplus occurs if the consumer is willing to pay more than the market price for a good or service.

77. (C) Because fertilizer is a factor of production for grapes, production costs for grapes will increase and thus Choice (C) is correct; the supply of grapes will decrease.

78. (A) Choice (A) is correct. An increase in demand will signal to suppliers to raise the prices of their products. If demand rises, then suppliers will raise their prices and a higher quantity will be sold.

79. (C) Choice (C) is correct. Since there was an increase in price for product X, a decrease in demand should result. If the demand for product Z increases as a result of an increase in the price of product X, then product Z is a substitute good.

80. (B) Choice (B) is correct. A price ceiling refers to the maximum price at which a producer is allowed to sell a good or service. This is usually instituted by law from the government and helps to ensure fair business practices. If credit card companies are regulated to institute a maximum amount on how much interest they can charge, then it is a price ceiling.

81. (B) Choice (B) is correct. A shortage is defined as a situation where the quantity demanded exceeds the quantity supplied. More and more people are demanding a particular good, but producers do not have an adequate supply of the good.

82. (A) Choice (A) is the best answer because it reflects the law of supply: producers are more willing and able to produce more of a good as price increases.

83. (A) Choice (A) is the best answer because the invisible hand is a reference to the ideas of economist Adam Smith in 1776. If producers act in their own self-interest, then society as a whole will benefit through trade and entrepreneurship. No government intervention is needed; the economy will correct itself in the long run.

84. (D) Choice (D) is correct. The determinants of supply refer to the external factors that influence supply. If these determinants change, then the supply curve will shift to the left or the right. Some of the determinants of supply are price, available technology, the number of producers in the market, and taxes imposed by the government.

85. (D) Choice (D) is correct. A surplus exists when the quantity supplied is greater than the quantity demanded. A surplus is another way of saying there is an excess of supply. Choice (B) is incorrect because the equilibrium point is the intersection between supply and demand, where the supply equals the demand. Choice (C) is incorrect because it refers to the percentage of income distribution in a society.

86. (B) Choice (B) is correct. Establishing an effective price floor will create a market surplus because suppliers will produce more than consumers demand. If a market surplus already exists, the size of the surplus will increase.

87. (A) Choice (A) is correct. Economies of scale refers to the downward part of the long-run average total cost (LRAC) curve where LRAC falls as plant size rises; constant returns to scale refers to changes in output by the same proportion as a change in input; and diseconomies of scale refers to the upward sloping part of the LRAC where firms see an increase in marginal cost as output increases. Choice (A) is the best answer because it reflects these definitions.

88. (C) Choice (C) is the best answer because if there are too few substitutes and little time for changes to production to be made, then demand is said to be inelastic. Therefore, substitutes and time are determinants of elasticity.

89. (B) Choice (B) is correct. The supply of wheat increases, so if demand doesn't change, the wheat price falls. With inexpensive wheat on the market serving as a substitute good for corn, the corn price also falls.

90. (A) Choice (A) is correct. The elasticity formula is percent change in quantity divided by percent change in price. If the answer is greater than 1, the good is said to be price sensitive. If the answer is less than 1, the good is said not to be price sensitive. Because 4/2 = 2, the good would be price elastic.

91. (D) Choice (D) is correct. An increase in demand for hamburgers shifts the demand curve for buns to the right and the price of buns rises.

92. (A) Choice (A) is correct. Dead weight loss refers to the lost net benefit to society caused by a movement from competitive market equilibrium. When price increases above the equilibrium because of taxes, a dead weight loss occurs.

93. (A) Choice (A) is correct. Dead weight loss refers to the lost net benefit to society caused by a movement from competitive market equilibrium. When the quantity produced is above the market equilibrium quantity, dead weight loss occurs.

94. (A) Choice (A) is correct. The law of diminishing marginal utility states that as a person increases consumption of a good, satisfaction or utility decreases with each marginal consumption of the good. For example, say you really liked hot dogs and you started eating them every day. With consumption of each hot dog, there would come a point where you would like them less and less.

95. (C) Choice (C) is correct. The price elasticity formula is percent change in quantity divided by percent change in price. If the answer is greater than 1, the good is said to be price sensitive. If the answer is less than 1, the good is said not to be price sensitive. However, if the answer is zero, then the demand is completely independent from the price. Consumers will purchase the good regardless of the price.

96. (B) Choice (B) is correct. If joint demand exists for two goods, they are complementary goods.

97. (A) Choice (A) is correct. The price increase for bell peppers would shift the demand curve for artichokes to the right. A demand shift from D1 to D2 is a move to the right, the other choices are moves to the left.

98. (C) Choice (C) is correct. A price drop for tomatoes causes a larger shift in artichoke demand, so tomatoes are a better substitute for artichokes.

99. (A) Choice (A) is correct. If a business owns plants at various stages of production, then it is a vertically integrated firm. This means that a business expands to different points along the same production path.

100. (A) Choice (A) is the best answer because spillover costs refer to the additional costs to a society and not to part of the supply curve from the production of a good. The government would intervene either in the form of a tax on producers to limit production or to internalize the spillover cost into the supply curve.

101. (C) Choice (C) is correct. In a monopolistic competition, product differentiation is utilized to make a product stand out from its competitors. For example, there are many similarities between iPhone and BlackBerry smartphones, but there are very subtle differences that appeal to different consumers.

102. (A) Choice (A) is correct. In a monopolistic competition, product differentiation is utilized to make a product stand out from its competitors. There are not as many competitors in a monopolistic competition as compared to a perfect competition, where there are many. As a result, the monopolistic competitive firm must differentiate its product to increase consumer demand. An Italian restaurant is an example of a monopolistic competition. Your neighborhood may have more than one Italian restaurant, but one may have that "secret ingredient" in their sauce that you just love, or other dishes that the other restaurants do not offer. Such a business differentiates its product so that it can stand out from other competitors.

103. (B) Choice (B) is correct. A franchise pays a licensing fee to another firm for rights to produce branded goods or services.

104. (A) Choice (A) is correct. The law of diminishing returns states that as more and more units are added to production, there is a point where the marginal revenue product declines. In the short run, marginal cost is low, but as more and more is produced, marginal cost increases.

105. (C) Choices (A), (B), (D), and (E) are all variable production inputs because they can easily be influenced and changed in the short run. Choice (C) is the best answer because human capital refers to the skills and education a worker brings to the production of a product. This is not as easily manipulated by producers in a firm.

106. (C) Choice (C) is correct. This question is very straightforward. If a variable production input—an input that is not a part of fixed costs—increases, then the marginal cost will increase as well. For example, suppose a plant adds a new machine that uses more electricity than the other machines in the plant. This is an increase in the factors of production, and the firm will respond by increasing the price of the product to cover the additional cost in electricity.

107. (A) Choice (A) is the best answer. Regulators may require average cost pricing in exchange for granting a natural monopoly to a firm.

108. (B) Choice (B) is correct. A monopolistic competition refers to a market structure with many firms producing a differentiated product with easy entry into the market. Choice (A) is wrong because it refers to a natural monopoly. Choice (C) is incorrect because it refers to an oligopoly. Choice (D) is incorrect because it refers to a perfect competition. Choice (E) is incorrect because it refers to a monopoly.

109. (A) Choice (A) is correct. Economic profit is the difference between total revenue and total economic cost. Economic profit incorporates opportunity costs, whereas accounting profit does not.

110. (D) Choice (D) is correct. Diseconomies of scale exist on the upward sloping part of the LRAC curve. In the long run, firms see increasing costs as production increases.

111. (E) Choice (E) is the best answer. Constant returns to scale refers to changes in output by the same proportion as a change in input. It is the point between economies of scale and diseconomies of scale.

112. (B) Choice (B) is the best answer. Economies of scale refers to an increase in the efficiency of a production as production levels increase. Choice (A) is incorrect because specialization usually does not result in a decrease in profits. Choice (C) is incorrect because specialization coincides with a decrease in production costs. Choice (D) is incorrect because both changes in input are the same as a change in output, so it tends to be a straight line on the LRAC curve. Choice (E) is incorrect because diseconomies of scale refers to an increase in marginal cost when production increases.

113. (C) Choice (C) is correct. An oligopoly is a market structure where there are a small number of interdependent firms producing either a standardized or differentiated product with barriers to entry. Firms in an oligopoly have significant pricing power. Choice (A) is incorrect because it refers to a natural monopoly. Choice (B) is incorrect because it refers to a monopoly. Choice (D) is incorrect because it refers to a monopolistic competition. Choice (E) is incorrect because it refers to a perfect competition.

114. (A) Choice (A) is correct. This diagram represents a total cost curve. You should know the differences between the total cost curve and the average total cost curve. This is a total cost curve because of its shape: the curve intercepts the Y-axis positively, which indicates fixed costs; and the rest of the curve illustrates fixed costs plus variable costs.

115. (A) Choice (A) is correct. In general, economists say that firms do not go out of business in the short run. They must pay their fixed costs. However, firms may shut down and not pay their variable costs. If Mr. Ray is considering shutting down his business, then the two most important factors he should analyze are average variable cost (AVC) and marginal revenue (MR). The firm will stay open if MR = AVC or MR > AVC. If marginal revenue, the same as price, is equal to average variable costs, then firms could shut down and pay only their fixed costs. If MR < AVC, then firms may shut down.

116. (D) Choice (D) is the best answer. Monopolistic competition allows firms to earn short-run economic profits but not long-run economic profits.

117. (B) Choice (B) is correct. At the point where price is greater than average total costs, more firms will enter the market due to the attractiveness of the business venture. This is so because both fixed and variable costs are being covered by the price. As a result, prices will go down as more and more firms enter the market. Remember, in a perfectly competitive market, economic profit in the long run is zero.

118. (C) Choice (C) is correct. The movie theater is using price discrimination to maximize profit by setting different ticket prices for two groups of customers.

119. (A) Choice (A) is correct. A monopoly is a market structure where one firm is the producer for a good or service with very few substitutes and many barriers to entry. There is virtually no competition in a monopoly market structure.

120. (E) Choice (E) is correct. If an owner of a firm is trying to decide whether to shut down, then analyzing marginal revenue (MR) and average variable cost (AVC) will help. The firm will stay open if MR = AVC or MR > AVC. If marginal revenue, the same as price, is equal to average variable costs, then firms could shut down and pay only their fixed costs. If MR < AVC, then firms may shut down.

121. (A) Choice (A) is correct. In any competitive market, the profit-maximizing point is where MR = MC. If MR is greater than MC, then the firm would make a profit. If MC is greater than MR, then the firm would be losing money.

122. (D) A perfectly competitive firm in the long run shows a profit of zero after more and more firms enter the market. Choice (D) is the best choice because as more and more firms enter the market, and existing markets adjust their size, the price will decrease and all firms will only be making a normal profit.

123. (D) If new firms enter a market, the firms already competing in the market will lose market power so Choice (D) is the best answer.

124. (C) Collusion refers to rival firms all agreeing to disrupt the market equilibrium price of their product. This often occurs in an oligopoly. For example, the firms may all agree to alter the supply of the product to raise prices on the market. Choice (C) is the best answer because this is an often-used business tactic for cartels.

125. (C) Choice (C) is the best answer because an oligopoly is a market structure where there are a small number of interdependent firms producing either a standardized or differentiated product with barriers to entry. Very often, the firms may all agree to alter the supply of the product to raise prices in the market.

126. (D) If the price of a good increases, consumers lose purchasing power. If the good is a significant part of a consumer's income or budget, then a change in price will be greatly felt. Choice (D) is the best answer because purchasing fruit does not make up a significant percentage of a person's income or budget as compared to buying and maintaining a boat.

127. (B) Choice (B) is the best answer because a school can hire teaching assistants very easily in the short run. Long-run adjustments are major and significant changes to a firm, such as plant size and investing in human capital.

128. (A) Choice (A) is correct. A perfect competition is a market structure where many firms are producing very similar products, prices are established through supply and demand, and there is freedom to enter and exit the market.

129. (C) Choice (C) is correct. A monopoly can earn an economic profit in the long term because other firms cannot enter the market. In monopolistic competition, firms can easily enter the market so profit will be normal in the long term.

130. (C) Choice (C) is correct. If marginal revenue (MR), the same as price, is equal to average variable costs (AVC), then firms could shut down and pay only their total fixed costs (TFC). If firms shut down in the short run, then AVC does not need to be paid, only TFC.

131. (C) Choice (C) is correct. Since a monopoly is the sole producer of a product, the firm will charge an increased price as compared to a perfect competition, where price is established through supply and demand. Remember, in a monopoly, there is no competition, so firms will always charge a higher price.

132. (E) Choice (E) is the best answer because a perfect competition is a market structure where many firms are producing very similar products, prices are established through supply and demand, and there is freedom to enter and exit the market.

133. (A) Choice (A) is correct. There are many different types of smartphones on the market produced by many different firms. Although they are similar in many ways (i.e., you can make a phone call, send a text, and surf the Internet), product differentiation offers variety. Remember, if you see product differentiation, then a monopolistic competition or an oligopoly is being discussed.

134. (D) Choice (D) is correct. A natural monopoly is a market structure where it is beneficial for one firm to control the production of a good or service. For example, natural gas and the water authority work most efficiently and with the greatest benefit if there is a natural monopoly. It would be too complicated and at a great cost if competitive markets began running separate lines to households for gas and water.

135. (C) Choice (C) is the best answer because tobacco is a cost of production for cigarettes. If the price increases for a cost of production, then firms must increase their price to keep making a profit on producing the good.

136. (A) Choice (A) is the best answer because a consumer surplus is the difference between what a consumer is willing and able to pay and the actual market price. If the consumer was willing to pay more for the product than the established market price, then there is a consumer surplus.

137. (E) Choice (E) is the best answer. Two of the major characteristics of a monopolistic competition are product differentiation and advertising. Since product differentiation exists in a monopolistic competition, firms must advertise why their product is different and better than the products of their competitors.

138. (C) Choice (C) is correct. The goal of any firm is to make a profit with the products it is producing and selling. In a perfectly competitive market, there are no barriers to entry into the market. When a product is profitable for a perfectly competitive firm, it exists only in the short run. In the long run, profits are zero because of other firms entering the market.

139. (C) If more and more firms are exiting the market, then costs must be greater than price. Choice (C) is the best answer because it shows that price is less than average total cost (ATC) in a perfectly competitive market structure.

140. (A) Choice (A) is correct. Remember that a monopolist is the only producer of a good or service and has no competition. Therefore, the firm may raise the price higher than marginal costs. All firms will maximize profit where marginal revenue (MR) equals marginal cost (MC), but a monopolist will support a higher price than the MC.

141. (B) Choice (B) is correct. An oligopoly and a monopoly have barriers to entry into the market. A perfect competition and a monopolistic competition are market structures that have ease of entry into the market.

142. (C) Choice (C) is the best answer because allocative efficiency is achieved if price (P) equals marginal cost (MC). Choice (B) is incorrect because the government would not allow P to be greater than MC. Choices (A) and (D) represent allocative inefficiency.

143. (A) Choice (A) is the best answer. Marginal utility is defined as the additional satisfaction or utility a consumer receives from consuming one additional unit of a good. Choice (B) is incorrect because it refers to the marginal revenue cost. Choice (C) is incorrect because it refers to the marginal propensity to save. Choice (D) is incorrect because it describes marginal cost. Choice (E) is incorrect because it describes marginal cost.

144. (B) Choice (B) is the best answer. The law of diminishing marginal utility states that as a person increases consumption of a good, satisfaction or utility decreases with each marginal consumption of the good.

145. (B) When most people say the word *profit*, they are referring to accounting profit, calculated as the difference between total revenue and total explicit cost. Economic profit, however, calculates the opportunity cost (implicit cost). Choice (B) is the best answer.

146. (B) Choice (B) is the best answer because the diagram illustrates price equal to marginal revenue. This is true in a perfect competition.

147. (A) Choice (A) is the best answer because at any other level the firm runs the possibility of producing too much or too little, which would raise revenue or incur a cost.

148. (B) Choice (B) is correct. Price discrimination refers to a systematic pricing system that charges different prices to different groups of people. However, the firm will still ensure that the maximum price that these different people are willing to pay is utilized.

149. (A) Choice (A) is correct. Price discrimination allows firms to receive every dollar available from their customers. If a firm can successfully identify specific groups of people and ensure that customers do not resell their product to other consumers, then price discrimination would be successful. An example would be selling movie tickets in a theater. There are different prices for shows at different times, and different prices for different types of customers: adult, child, and senior citizen.

150. (D) Choice (D) is correct. Even though company Z does not own all the farmland used in the production of tobacco, it owns a significant majority. It now controls most of the farmland used in the production of tobacco. This shows that company Z is attempting to establish a monopoly by controlling one of the factors of production (land). Choice (A) is incorrect because all businesses wish to increase profits, and it does not fully answer the question. Choice (B) is incorrect because an oligopoly refers to a small number of very large firms; this question refers only to company Z. Choice (C) is incorrect because even though it is correct that the profit-maximizing point is where MR = MC, it does not relate to the scenario in the question.

151. (C) Choice (C) is correct. You should be aware of the graphical representation of profit for all market structures. This graph represents the profit of a monopolistically competitive firm. The shaded area represents profit because the price level is more than the average total cost (ATC). Since the ATC represents the total cost divided by the output, if the price is higher than this number, then the firm is making a profit.

152. (C) Choice (C) is correct. With no entry or exit barriers, firms will enter the market under monopolistic competition until all firms are earning a normal economic profit.

153. (D) Choice (D) is correct. Game theory examines the relationships between participants in a specific model structure and attempts to predict their actions. This is useful for studying oligopolies because they consist of very large firms that are interdependent companies, producing either a standardized or differentiated product with barriers to entry.

154. (E) Choice (E) is the best answer because establishing an ineffective price ceiling will not influence quantity demanded or supplied. It only ensures that producers will not exceed a specific price for their product, thus protecting consumers.

155. (A) Choice (A) is correct. If the supply curve for grape jelly shifts to the right, the price of grape jelly will fall. This will increase demand for peanut butter because it is a complementary good.

156. (E) Choice (E) is correct. Remember that for all market structures, the profit-maximizing point is where MR = MC.

157. (B) Item I is not a part of a market system because it describes the operations of a traditional economy. Item III is not part of a market system because it describes a command economy. Choice (B) is correct because Item II describes the interactions between consumers and producers.

158. (D) Price leadership refers to a firm that is a leader among its competitors and sets the market price; others will follow along because they wish to hold on to their market share. Choice (D) is the best answer because an oligopoly fits this description.

159. (E) Choice (E) is correct. Limited liability refers to the notion that what a person is liable for in a business investment does not exceed the amount of the original investment. If you start a business with limited liability but go bankrupt, then you would not lose your personal assets. It is beneficial for all types of businesses.

160. (C) Choice (C) is the best answer because if something is implicit, then it is not blatantly seen outright. An opportunity cost is an excellent example of an implicit cost. Choice (A) is incorrect because it describes explicit costs. Choice (B) is incorrect because it describes total variable costs. Choice (D) is incorrect because it describes average variable costs.

161. (D) Choice (D) is the best answer because the complement effect refers to an increase or decrease in demand for a product that works with another product. For example, if the demand for tennis rackets increases, so will the demand for tennis balls. This reflects a direct relationship, whereas all the other choices reflect an inverse relationship.

162. (D) Choice (D) is correct. An increase in technology is a major change in the factors of production. If technology increases, then production output will increase as well. This will result in greater profits. However, since this is a perfectly competitive market, price will remain the same.

163. (A) Choice (A) is correct. Tacos are a better substitute for burritos, so the cross-price elasticity of demand will be higher.

164. (A) Choice (A) is the best answer because if a firm is utilizing its resources to allocative efficiency, then price (P) will equal marginal cost (MC). Keep in mind the opposite notion: since monopolies are notoriously inefficient, they operate where P is greater than MC.

165. (B) Choice (B) is correct. Corn oil is less substitutable for olive oil so its cross-price elasticity of demand will be lower.

166. (B) Choice (B) is correct. A cartel, which is a form of an oligopoly, is a market structure where there are a small number of interdependent firms, producing either a standardized or differentiated product with barriers to entry. Since these firms work together to establish prices and control supply and demand, there is always an incentive for a firm to cheat to earn a greater profit than its competitors.

167. (A) Choice (A) is correct. Dead weight loss refers to the lost net benefit to society caused by a movement from competitive market equilibrium. In other words, the people who would purchase the good who have more marginal benefit than marginal price are not purchasing the product. For a monopoly, this occurs when price is greater than marginal cost.

168. (E) Choice (E) is the best answer because P = MR = MC = ATC represents a perfectly competitive firm.

169. (A) Choice (A) is correct. Price taking refers to firms that establish their price through the market forces of supply and demand. Since oligopolies are very large firms and work together to control supply and demand, they are price setters.

170. (A) Choice (A) is correct. The reason a monopoly can charge a higher price is because there are no competitors in the market. If a firm is the sole producer of a product, it will charge a higher price. Choices (B) and (D) are incorrect.

171. (C) Price elasticity of demand is extremely useful because it helps firms and economists predict consumer behavior if there is a change in price. Choice (C) is the best answer.

172. (B) Choice (B) is correct. Remember, an effective price ceiling will always be demarcated below the market equilibrium price on a supply-and-demand chart.

173. (A) Calculating the cross-elasticity refers to the measurement taken of how sensitive the consumption of one good is to the change in price of another good. Choice (A) is the best answer.

174. (A) Choice (A) is correct. A normal profit is described as another way of saying a firm is earning an economic profit of zero. It earned the same amount that it would earn from the next best use of its resources, so it also earned an economic profit. This is so because normal profit and economic profit consider opportunity costs.

175. (C) Choice (C) is the best answer because if producing a product is profitable, more and more firms will enter the market due to the ease of entry. Remember, in the long run, the economic profits of a perfectly competitive firm will be zero.

176. (E) Choice (E) is the best answer because MR = MC represents the profit-maximizing point for all market structures. If a firm is operating at this point, then all resources are being utilized efficiently.

177. (E) Choice (E) is the best answer because it describes price leadership, where one firm is a leader among its competitors and sets the market price, and others will follow along because they wish to hold on to their market share. This is very true for oligopolies.

178. (A) Choice (A) is correct. Remember, the profit-maximizing point will always be MR = MC for any market structure, even a cartel.

179. (A) Choice (A) is the best answer because a restriction to how many firms enter the market would allow a greater opportunity for profit. Choices (B) and (E) are incorrect because the opposite is true due to barriers to entry. Choice (C) is incorrect because price discrimination is unrelated. Choice (D) is incorrect because it is unrelated.

180. (B) The correct choice is (B) because the income effect describes the relationship between income and demand: as a person's income increases or decreases, it will increase or decrease demand for a product. Choice (A) is incorrect because it describes the substitution effect. Choice (C) is incorrect because it describes marginal utility. Choices (D) and (E) are incorrect because they are not related to the income effect.

181. (B) Remember that a perfectly competitive firm in the long run will have economic profits of zero. Normal profit will equal economic profit.

182. (D) Choice (D) is correct. This graph illustrates the total revenue curve, and also provides information about changes in marginal revenue.

183. (A) Choice (A) is correct. If economies of scale exist, average cost falls as output increases. Larger firms have higher output than smaller firms so they receive more benefit from economies of scale.

184. (C) Choice (C) is correct. A price increase from $1 to $1.25 is a 25 percent increase. Quantity demanded fell 50 percent. 50%/25% = 2, which is above 1, so demand for golf balls is elastic.

185. (A) Choice (A) is correct. Average total cost (ATC) is the total cost divided by the output. If the ATC equals price (P), then firms will make an economic profit of zero.

186. (C) Choice (C) is correct. Market power refers to the ability of a firm to set prices above the perfectly competitive level. A perfectly competitive firm does not have market power because prices are determined through supply and demand. Therefore, a perfect competition is a price taker. A monopoly market structure fits perfectly with the idea of market power because as the only producer of the good, it increases prices above where MR = MC.

187. (B) Choice (B) is correct. When monopolistic competition exists, firms sell differentiated products. Since these products aren't complete replacements for one another, the firms have some market power.

188. (D) Choice (D) is correct. In any market structure, the profit-maximizing point is where marginal revenue equals marginal cost. In a perfectly competitive market, price will equal marginal revenue. Choice (A) is incorrect, although deceiving, because only in the long run will a perfect competition have a zero profit. This is because more and more firms enter the market, cutting price and profit. Choice (B) is incorrect because the question shows that the firm is profit maximizing and would result in more firms entering, not leaving, the market. Choice (C) is incorrect because this is a business tactic of an oligopoly.

189. (A) In any market structure the profit-maximizing point is where marginal revenue equals marginal cost. Choice (B) is incorrect because if the revenue product of labor (MRP) is less than the wages paid to workers, then the firm will respond by laying off workers. Choice (C) is incorrect because average fixed costs are costs that must be paid regardless if the firm is making a profit or losing money. Choice (D) is incorrect because economic decisions are not followed through if the marginal cost is greater than the marginal benefit.

190. (A) Choice (A) is correct. A patent is a grant given by the government allowing the patent holder the sole right to produce and sell a product for a set period of time. If a producer is the only producer of a product, then it is a monopoly.

191. (B) Choice (B) is correct. Economies of scale refers to a decrease in ATC as quantity increases. Choice (A) is incorrect because it describes diseconomies of scale. Choice (C) is incorrect because if quantity decreases, ATC will not necessarily decrease. Choice (D) is incorrect because it describes the profit-maximizing point and is unrelated to economies of scale in the short run. Choice (E) is incorrect because it refers to elasticity.

192. (A) Choice (A) is correct. The price fell 40 percent and train ridership (quantity demanded) rose 20 percent. 20%/40% = 0.5, which is below 1, so demand for train tickets is inelastic.

193. (D) Choice (D) is correct. If any price increase would cause quantity demanded to fall to zero, demand is perfectly elastic. This usually occurs when items have a legally fixed value; a $10 bill is always worth $10.

194. (B) Choice (B) is the best answer. Demand for Giffen goods does increase when the price rises, but Giffen goods are inferior goods. Veblen goods are luxury goods used for conspicuous consumption. Consumers buy them to show off their wealth. Thus, a luxury handbag is a Veblen good if a higher price results in higher demand.

195. (D) Choice (D) is the best answer. If an inferior good is a necessity and substitutes are not available, a worker may demand more of the inferior good and fewer normal goods if the price of the inferior good increases. For example, the shoe store worker could buy more rice and give up hot sauce used to season the rice. Therefore, the income effect affects demand more strongly than the substitution effect, indicating the presence of a Giffen good.

196. (B) Choice (B) is correct. If a perfect substitute is available for a good, increasing the price of the good will cause quantity demanded to fall to zero.

197. (A) The correct choice is (A). Duration (time) affects price elasticity because a consumer may not be able to find a substitute good in the short term but can find a substitute good after more time has passed. Thus, demand for a good may be more elastic over longer time frames.

198. (B) Choice (B) is correct. If fewer substitute products were available, the demand curve would shift to the right, not the left.

199. (E) Choice (E) is correct. The first four factors would reduce production costs, shifting the supply curve to the right.

200. (C) Choice (C) is correct. Crop price supports are an example of a price floor. They would not change the equilibrium price or quantity and would result in oversupply and a dead weight loss, as quantity supplied would be higher than quantity demanded.

201. (C) Choice (C) is correct. A dining facility expansion would take place over the long term so it won't increase short-term revenue. The other inputs can be adjusted during the short term.

202. (A) Choice (A) is the best answer. In a market economy without rent control laws, apartments supplied would equal apartments demanded at point C. Rent control laws would cause apartments supplied to decrease toward A2, while apartments demanded would increase toward B2. Applicants would outnumber available rental units, resulting in a housing shortage.

203. (A) The size of a dead weight loss can be calculated by measuring the area between quantity demanded, quantity supplied, and equilibrium price/quantity. Choice (A) is correct, the dead weight loss caused by a housing shortage would be represented by the area inside the triangle bounded by points A2, B2, and C.

204. (D) The correct choice is (D). The soda manufacturer set the price of a soda can at $5 and limited quantity to 200, while the equilibrium price would be $2. So the soda manufacturer collects an economic profit of $600 by limiting quantity.

205. (B) The correct choice is (B). Choice (C) is the soda manufacturer's economic profit.

206. (C) Choice (C) is correct. The shift would indicate that the soda manufacturer lost its monopoly.

207. (A) Choice (A) is correct. Rubber is a variable production input, not a capital good included in fixed costs, so a change in its price doesn't affect fixed costs.

208. (C) Choice (C) is correct. Joe is earning an accounting profit of $40,000 but would earn $50,000 as an engineer, so he incurs an economic loss of $10,000.

209. (C) Choice (C) is the best answer. In the second year, the shoe store is earning zero economic profit because Joe's profit as an owner equals the wage he would earn at a company. Thus, the market has likely reached long-run equilibrium.

210. (B) Choice (B) is correct. The furniture company achieved economies of scale by opening up the second plant because its first plant became more profitable as well.

211. (C) Choice (C) is the best answer. The auto manufacturer earns $300,000 from three plants, so each plant produces $100,000 in profit. Its first plant was producing $100,000 in profit by itself, so the auto manufacturer achieved constant returns to scale.

212. (B) Choice (C) is correct. Competition ensures that prices will be controlled through the market forces of supply and demand. If a monopoly exists, that firm may set a much higher price than in a perfectly competitive market. If competition exists, then it will increase the total welfare and benefit society.

213. (A) Choice (A) is the best answer. The auto parts manufacturer achieved economies of scale. It also achieved increasing returns to scale so Choices (D) and (E) are incorrect.

214. (C) Choice (C) is correct. Economic profit is equal to accounting profit minus the profit that would be earned if resources (in this case, the owner's skills) were put to the next best possible use.

215. (A) This market is an oligopoly. Few manufacturers and long-run economic profits are the distinguishing features of this market. Product differentiation could also indicate monopolistic competition and does not always exist in an oligopoly.

216. (A) Choice (A) is correct. The next best possible use of Nate's skills pays $80,000 so opening a restaurant that earns an economic profit of $60,000 results in an economic profit of –$20,000, or an economic loss.

217. (B) Choice (B) is the best answer. The supply curve will shift to the left and a smaller quantity will be sold at higher prices.

218. (A) Choice (A) is correct. A group of firms in an oligopoly may form a cartel to set the price for their goods, which is collusion. Because these firms set the price, they have market power. This is not an example of a monopoly because more than one oil company is in the market.

219. (A) Choice (A) is the best answer. There are more apple farms so substitutes for any farm's apples are more widely available, thus demand should be more price elastic.

220. (B) Choice (B) is the best answer. This market can be described as a perfect competition. While demand is likely downward sloping for the market as a whole, there are many peanut farms selling undifferentiated peanuts so an individual farm's decisions don't affect the market price. Thus, demand for an individual peanut farm is perfectly elastic.

221. (E) Choice (E) is the best answer. To reduce costs, a firm can shut down production in the short run, lay off workers, or reduce its raw material purchases. Refinancing corporate bonds would change the firm's capital structure, which is considered a long-run decision.

222. (B) Choice (B) is the best answer. If a good increases in price, a complementary good will also increase in price.

223. (D) The correct choice is (D). On the left side of the cost curve, the toy manufacturer's average cost decreases as production rises because fixed cost is applied to a greater production quantity. When the toy manufacturer's production quantity increases beyond the trough of the cost curve, diminishing marginal returns have a larger impact on average cost than the decrease in fixed cost and average cost rises.

224. (A) Choice (A) is the best answer because firms in an oligopoly consider other firms' responses to business decisions, while monopolistic competition includes many small firms whose decisions don't greatly impact each other.

225. (C) Choice (C) is correct. The auto manufacturer's next best choice is shutting down for an accounting profit of –$40,000. If it produces tires, its accounting profit is –$10,000. Thus, it earns an economic profit of $30,000.

226. (B) Choice (B) is correct. The cable companies have an oligopoly and may be colluding to control the market.

227. (C) Choice (C) is the best answer. When there are many sellers and few buyers, the market is an oligopsony.

228. (B) Choice (B) is the best answer. The steel manufacturer is a monopsony.

229. (B) Choice (B) is the best answer. Charging different prices to viewers in different countries is price discrimination.

230. (A) Choice (A) is correct. Firm A would earn a profit of $25 if it lowered prices and firm B raised prices. Firm B would then lose $5.

231. (A) Choice (A) is correct. If firms A and B both raise prices, each firm earns a profit of $10.

232. (D) Choice (D) is the best answer. In an oligopoly, a firm may use a payoff matrix to consider other firms' decisions when setting prices.

233. (A) Choice (A) is the best answer. Defecting always results in a higher payoff than cooperating, so a firm always has an incentive to defect. Thus, the Nash equilibrium is for both firms to defect.

234. (C) Choice (C) is the best answer. An individual oil producer can increase its profit by increasing quantity supplied because the cartel is supplying less oil than the market is willing to buy. Thus, the oil producer has an incentive to defect from the cartel, although the cartel may respond by ejecting the oil producer for violating the agreement.

235. (D) Choice (D) is the best answer. Buying ads has a payoff of $70 or $40, while not buying ads has a payoff of $50 or $30, so the dominant strategy for Joey's is buying ads.

236. (A) Choice (A) is correct. Joey's and Betty's both earn $40 if they each buy ads. They would each earn $50 if neither restaurant bought ads.

237. (C) Choice (C) is correct. Max incurs opportunity costs of $100,000 (his salary) and $5,000 (his dividend income) to earn $120,000 from the bakery. Thus, his economic profit is $120,000 – $100,000 – $5,000, or $15,000.

238. (B) The best choice is (B). A price floor will have no effect if it's set below the equilibrium price.

239. (A) Choice (A) is correct. Producer surplus is the area to the left of the supply curve and below the price equilibrium. The area above the price equilibrium and to the left of the demand curve is consumer surplus.

240. (A) Choice (A) is the best answer. If consumers expect lower auto prices, demand shifts to the left.

241. (C) Choice (C) is correct. If consumers expect higher auto prices, demand shifts to the right.

242. (D) Choice (D) is the best answer. There are no substitute goods for steak, so demand is likely less price elastic than it is for chicken, pork, and fish, products for which substitute goods are available.

243. (A) Choice (A) is the best answer. If P < ATC, firms won't earn a profit. A perfectly competitive market has low exit barriers, so firms will exit the market and the price will rise.

244. (C) Choice (C) is the best answer. The movie theater chain is a monopoly and a monopoly can reduce the size of the dead weight loss it creates by price discriminating.

245. (A) Choice (A) is the best answer. The auto manufacturer always earns the most profit by producing where MR = MC.

246. (D) Choice (D) is correct. The difference between market price ($40,000) and the price the automaker will accept for the car ($30,000) is $10,000.

247. (E) Choice (E) is correct. Consumer surplus is the price the consumer is willing to pay for a banana ($2.60) minus the market price of a banana ($2.25) which is $0.35.

248. (A) Choice (A) is correct. For the raspberry farm, MR = MC at $5. Thus, it should increase production to that output level to maximize profit. It should not increase production until MC equals the market price of $6 because MC would rise above MR if that happened.

249. (C) Choice (C) is the best answer because price discrimination would increase profits. Choice (A) isn't necessary because the firm already has a monopoly. Choices (B) and (D) are incorrect because MR should already equal MC. Choice (E) is illegal.

250. (A) Choice (A) is the best answer. The cruise line will earn a higher profit because of price discrimination. The cruise line is a monopoly so dead weight loss will decrease, quantity supplied will increase, and the cruise line will continue to earn an economic profit.

251. (B) Choice (B) is the best answer. If four firms have 80 percent market share, the market is an oligopoly, and firms would earn economic profit in the long run. Patents may prevent other firms from entering the market. Low construction costs, no collusion, and few economies of scale would result in low barriers to entry, so many firms would enter the market and a few firms would not have most of the market share.

252. (B) Choice (B) is correct. The auto manufacturer can't produce car windows if it produces car doors, so the money it would have earned by selling car windows is an implicit cost.

253. (C) Choice (C) is correct. The department store can currently sell the land for $1 million. The original price it paid for the land doesn't affect implicit cost.

254. (B) Choice (B) is correct. The next best use of the property earns $120,000 in profit. Therefore, accounting profit must increase from $100,000 to $120,000, a $20,000 increase, for the restaurant chain to earn a normal profit on the property.

255. (A) Choice (A) is correct. All market types other than perfect competition include inefficiencies that prevent firms from reaching allocative efficiency.

256. (B) Choice (B) is correct. If the price falls below the intervention price, the government begins buying goods in the market. This shifts the demand curve to the right.

257. (A) Choice (A) is correct. Dividing a 40 percent increase by a 20 percent increase results in a cross-price demand elasticity of 2. This result indicates that tomatoes and lettuce are substitute goods.

258. (B) Choice (B) is correct. If quantity demanded for blackberry jam divided by 20 percent equals –2, then quantity demanded must be –40 percent. This result indicates that blackberry jam and peanut butter are complementary goods.

259. (A) Choice (A) is correct. The price floor causes the price to shift from the equilibrium point to the point where the supply curve meets line A, resulting in a surplus. The size of the surplus is the area of the triangle bounded by the points where line A crosses the supply and demand curves and the equilibrium price point. This is considered a dead weight loss.

260. (B) Choice (B) is correct. A price ceiling represented by line B would result in a shortage represented by the area above line B and between the supply and demand curves. This is considered a dead weight loss.

261. (B) Choice (B) is correct. If the price of chicken increases 10 percent and cross-price elasticity of demand is 5, then quantity demanded for pork will increase 50 percent. The new quantity demanded for pork will be 10 + (10 × 50 percent), or 15.

262. (B) Choice (B) is correct. Dividing –20 percent by 50 percent results in cross-price demand elasticity of –0.4. Thus, bread and cheese are complementary goods.

263. (C) Choice (C) is correct. If the corn price rose 40 percent and cross-price elasticity of demand is 0.75, quantity demanded for wheat rose by 30 percent. If the new quantity demanded is 13, then the original quantity demanded was 10.

264. (A) Choice (A) is correct. Quantity demanded increased from 50 to 80, which is a 60 percent increase. Dividing 60 percent by 30 percent results in a price elasticity of demand of 2. These are substitute goods.

265. (B) Choice (B) is correct. The truck price increased 10 percent and quantity demanded for radios fell 30 percent, so price elasticity of demand for trucks and radios is –3. These are complementary goods.

266. (C) Choice (C) is correct. Dividing 5 percent by 20 percent results in a cross-price demand elasticity of 0.25. Thus, grapes and bananas are substitute goods.

267. (A) Choice (A) is correct. Price elasticity of supply is the change in quantity supplied divided by the change in price.

268. (E) Choice (E) is correct. If price elasticity of supply is 1, it is unitary elastic.

269. (B) Choice (B) is correct. If price elasticity of supply is zero, it is perfectly inelastic, or fixed.

270. (A) Choice (A) is the best answer. If factors of production are easy to obtain, supply will be more elastic and price elasticity of supply will be greater than 1.

271. (B) Choice (B) is the best answer. Price elasticity of supply increases over the long run because the manufacturer has more options available, such as expanding acres planted.

272. (A) Choice (A) is correct. Quantity supplied rose 50 percent and price increased 20 percent so price elasticity of supply for bell peppers is 2.5.

273. (E) Choice (E) is correct. Quantity supplied fell 15 percent and price fell 30 percent so price elasticity of supply for peaches is 0.5.

274. (B) Choice (B) is the best answer. The fashion retailer can easily adjust output, but the motorcycle manufacturer needs more time to adjust output. Thus, price elasticity of supply will be low for the fashion retailer and high for the motorcycle manufacturer.

275. (B) Choice (B) is the best answer. According to the law of supply, quantity supplied should decrease because suppliers will be less willing to produce the good.

276. (A) Choice (A) is correct. Income elasticity of demand is the percentage change in quantity demanded divided by the percentage change in income.

277. (A) Choice (A) is the best answer. The increased health care costs are an example of a negative externality resulting from increased soda demand. There is no evidence that production costs decreased or the government regulated the price of soda.

278. (B) Choice (B) is correct. Choice (C), consumer expectations, is a determinant of demand as well.

279. (A) Choice (A) is correct. The quantity of apples supplied doubles from 10 to 20 when the price doubles from $0.75 to $1.50, so apple supply is unitary elastic.

280. (C) Choice (C) is correct. Income elasticity of demand for oatmeal is –15 percent divided by 30 percent, or –0.5.

281. (A) Choice (A) is correct. When income elasticity of demand is zero, the good is a sticky good.

282. (C) Choice (C) is correct. The formula for the tax paid by the consumer is PES divided by (PES minus PED). This is 0.6/(0.6 – –0.2), or 0.6/0.8, which comes out to 0.75. Since the tax was $50, the consumer pays $50 × 0.75, or $37.50.

283. (B) Choice (B) is correct. The formula is 0.6/(0.6 – –0.4). This equals 0.6/1.0, or 0.6, so the car buyer pays 60 percent of the tariff.

284. (B) Choice (B) is the best answer. If supply is inelastic and demand is elastic, manufacturers can't raise prices or reduce quantity produced and must absorb a tax hike.

285. (C) Choice (C) is the best answer. When supply is elastic and demand is inelastic, a manufacturer can raise prices and make buyers pay the cost of a tax increase.

286. (C) Choice (C) is correct. The portion of medical benefits paid by the consumer can be calculated with the formula PES/(PES – PED) as well. Using the formula, the consumer share of medical benefit costs is 0.4/(0.4 – –0.6), or 0.4. The consumer pays 40 percent of the cost increase, which was 20 percent, so the increase in cost for the consumer is 8 percent.

287. (D) Choice (D) is correct. The portion of the tax burden absorbed by the manufacturer is –PED/(PES – PED). The clothing manufacturer pays –0.3/(0.9 – –0.3) percent of the tax, which is 25 percent. Since the tariff was 30 percent, clothing manufacturers must absorb a 7.5 percent cost increase.

288. (D) Choice (D) is the best answer. If the good is a necessity, demand will be inelastic. Choices (A) and (C) make supply inelastic, and Choices (B) and (E) make demand elastic. To pass on a tax increase, supply should be elastic and demand should be inelastic.

289. (C) The truck manufacturer absorbs a percentage of the tax increase equal to –PED/(PES – PED). In this example, the percentage is 1.0 (1.5 – –1.0), or 1.0/2.5, which is equal to 0.4. Because 0.4 × $10,000 = $4,000, Choice (C) is correct.

290. (C) The best answer is (C), reduce wages. If supply is inelastic and demand is elastic, a manufacturer can't force buyers to pay the tax by raising prices. The manufacturer would have to absorb the tax hike by reducing other expenses, such as wages.

291. (B) Choice (B) is correct. Good A and good B are perfect complements.

292. (B) Choice (B) is the best answer. If two goods are perfect complements, another unit of one good is useless without another unit of the other good. A left sandal has no utility without a right sandal.

293. (E) Choice (E) is the best answer. If consumption moves to a curve on the right, this indicates an increase in consumer income.

294. (B) Choice (B) is the best answer. These indifference curves are flat and parallel to one another, so good D and good E must be perfect substitutes.

295. (A) Choice (A) is correct. Because of decreasing marginal utility, an indifference curve is typically convex (although it may be flat) but will never be concave. Consumer indifference curves are based on the assumptions that budget constraints exist and reaching satiation or the bliss point, a point where the consumer would not prefer to increase consumption any further, is impossible.

296. (D) Choice (D) is correct. Both point C and point D are on indifference curve I2 so a consumer would be indifferent between the amount of hats and jackets available at both points.

297. (C) Choice (C) is correct. Point E is located on an indifference curve farther to the right than point D. This could occur if economic expansion resulted in higher consumer income. The other four choices involve shifts between points on the same indifference curve.

298. (A) Choice (A) is the best answer. Because the price of good A decreased, the consumer can select a mix of goods located on an indifference curve on the right.

299. (B) Choice (B) is the best answer. If consumption shifts to a curve on the left and quantity demanded for a good increases, it is an inferior good.

300. (A) Choice (A) is the best answer. Because the price of good D increased, the consumer must select a mix of goods located on an indifference curve on the left.

301. (A) Choice (A) is correct. The consumer can maximize utility by purchasing a mix of goods located at the point where the budget constraint line is tangent to the consumer indifference curve.

302. (B) Choice (B) is correct. The budget constraint line (demand) is tangent to the indifference curve at point B, so that is equilibrium consumption.

303. (A) Choice (A) is correct. Excess demand results in a shortage.

304. (B) Choice (B) is the best answer. Choice (C) is correct, but this describes the income effect.

305. (C) Choice (C) is the best answer. Choice (B) describes the substitution effect.

306. (A) Choice (A) is correct. Demand for a private good is the horizontal sum of each consumer's demand curve.

307. (A) Choice (A) is correct. An effective price ceiling would create a market shortage.

308. (D) Choice (D) is the best answer. If car manufacturers exited the market, the price of cars would rise. A higher car price would result in a lower quantity demanded, but demand for cars would not fall. The other choices would reduce car demand.

309. (C) Choice (C) is correct. Increased supply would reduce sugar beet prices, increasing quantity demanded. The other choices would result in higher demand for sugar beets.

310. (A) Choice (A) is correct. The number of buyers is not a determinant of supply and the number of producers is not a determinant of demand, but both factors affect elasticity.

311. (B) Choice (B) is correct. Perceived health benefits would increase demand for mushrooms, resulting in a higher quantity supplied, but wouldn't increase supply.

312. (C) Choice (C) is correct. The demand curve for strawberries would shift left, resulting in a lower quantity supplied, but supply wouldn't change.

313. (A) Choice (A) is correct. Dividing 50 percent by 10 percent results in a price elasticity of 5, which is greater than 1, so television set demand is price elastic.

314. (C) Choice (C) is correct. Demand for sunscreen will shift to the right, but sunscreen supply won't increase.

315. (A) Choice (A) is correct. Supply for alfalfa would shift to the left, but demand for alfalfa wouldn't change.

316. (A) Choice (A) is correct. Lower supply and higher demand will increase the market price, but there isn't enough information to determine what will happen to equilibrium quantity.

317. (C) Choice (C) is correct. Higher supply and higher demand will increase the equilibrium quantity, but the change in market price can't be determined.

318. (A) Choice (A) is correct. Dividing 10 percent by 40 percent results in a price elasticity of 0.25.

319. (E) Choice (E) is the best answer. All of these regulations could result in a dead weight loss, creating either a shortage or a surplus in the market.

320. (C) Choice (C) is correct. If the market equilibrium price and quantity match, the market does not have an effective price floor/ceiling or undersupply/oversupply. An ineffective price floor or ceiling could still be present though.

321. (D) The best answer is Choice (D), because the buyer is willing to pay less for each additional apple. While Choice (B) and Choice (E) would result in the same total price for three apples, these answers provide no evidence of declining utility.

322. (C) The best choice is (C). A partnership includes several owners who are each liable for the business.

323. (C) The best choice is (C). A corporation may have hundreds—or even thousands or millions—of owners. These owners are protected by limited liability. A partnership could also have hundreds of owners but lacks the limited liability protection of a corporation. An oligopoly is several firms dominating a market and does not refer to the firms' ownership structure.

324. (B) The best answer is Choice (B). Acquiring a competitor does not necessarily create a monopoly or an oligopoly, although it is a step in that direction. A sole proprietorship or a partnership may acquire a direct competitor.

325. (A) Choice (A) is the best answer. Spillover costs and negative externalities both refer to damage caused by the business to the community.

326. (E) Producers create positive externalities as well as negative externalities. A business may build a road that non-employees also use. A business that pays for employee training increases the productivity of the workforce as a whole. A manufacturer employs workers who spend money at nearby stores and restaurants. If a business buys phones for its employees, other people's phones become more valuable because they can be used to call more people.

327. (B) Choice (B) is the best answer. The question describes the orange farm industry as a market with perfect competition. Thus, the orange farms have low pricing power (they are price takers).

328. (B) The market for tax software is an oligopoly. Barriers to entry are already high and the tax software companies are already price makers. Oligopolies typically don't involve price competition. Buying the other firm would create a monopoly, and regulators could block the acquisition on antitrust grounds. When a market is an oligopoly, firms often respond to competitors' business decisions, so Choice (B) is the best answer.

329. (B) Choice (B) is the best answer. With many stores and unique products, the clothing market can be described as monopolistic competition, so clothing stores are likely to spend much of their revenue on ads.

330. (C) Choice (C) is the best answer. By granting the water company a natural monopoly, water can be delivered efficiently without incurring excess infrastructure costs. Regulators often control pricing policy for firms with natural monopolies.

331. (B) Choice (B) is correct. The kinked demand curve for the gas station indicates an oligopoly, so the gas station would collect the most revenue at the price equilibrium point, B.

332. (D) Choice (D) is correct. The gas station would have to sell gasoline at a lower price to keep its market share if another gas station was offering gasoline for less than the equilibrium price, so the gas stations would be engaged in a price war.

333. (B) Choice (B) is the best answer. The price equilibrium is $2 per gallon so a price of $2.50 is above this point. In an oligopoly, a firm's demand curve is elastic above the price equilibrium point but inelastic below it. If the gas station was selling gasoline for a price above the equilibrium point, other firms could capture much of its market share by offering gasoline at a lower price.

334. (C) Choice (C) is the best answer. Because of the kinked demand curve, the gas station won't change its price because of minor fluctuations in raw material or labor costs, so the price is "sticky." Major fluctuations will result in a new equilibrium price point.

335. (C) Choice (C) is correct. The equilibrium price is $80 and the average cost is $60, so the firm earns $20 in economic profit for each golf club. If it sells 100 golf clubs, it earns $2,000.

336. (A) Choice (A) is the best answer. Lower consumer interest would reduce the equilibrium price for golf clubs but wouldn't increase production costs. An equipment breakdown would result in higher production costs but wouldn't reduce the equilibrium price. Increased competition over time explains both the increase in manufacturing costs (raw materials would actually become more expensive because more golf club manufacturers would demand them) and the fall in equilibrium price (price competition among golf club companies would result in a lower price for golf clubs).

337. (C) Choice (C) is correct. Cross-licensing the patents gives both software companies a way to prevent other firms from entering the market.

338. (B) Choice (B) is correct. Regulators grant a drug company a monopoly through a patent, but the patent will eventually expire. A natural monopoly held by a utility is often granted by regulators but doesn't end after a fixed period of time.

339. (A) Choice (A) is correct. If the pharmaceutical firm invents a new drug, it will get a monopoly on the new drug and can keep earning an economic profit. Once the patent on the existing drug expires, other firms (generic drug manufacturers) will enter the market, so the pharmaceutical firm will lose its opportunity to make an economic profit on that drug.

340. (A) Choice (A) is correct. Diseconomies of scale result in lower production efficiency.

341. (C) Choice (C) is correct. The apple farm would lose its customers if it raised the price of apples because its apples are a commodity. The apple farm can sell all of its apples so cutting the price wouldn't improve sales, and MC should already equal MR. A unique apple cultivar would be a differentiated product, resulting in monopolistic competition instead of perfect competition, which would give the apple firm an opportunity to earn an economic profit.

342. (D) Choice (D) is correct. The equilibrium price and quantity can be calculated with algebra. The quantity supplied will equal quantity demanded at equilibrium, and the supply price will equal the demand price. Let $10 + 4Q = 80 - 3Q$, then $10 = Q$. $P = 10 + (4 \times 10) = 50$.

343. (B) Choice (B) is correct. Let $80 + 6Q = 400 - 10Q$. Then $16Q = 320$ so $Q = 20$. $P = 80 + (6 \times 20) = 200$.

344. (D) Choice (D) is correct. Lower supply and lower demand will reduce equilibrium quantity, but the change in market price can't be determined.

345. (B) Choice (B) is correct. The price of an input fell, which will increase supply. Demand also fell. This will result in a lower market price, but the change in equilibrium quantity can't be determined.

346. (C) Choice (C) is correct. The equilibrium price and quantity can be calculated with algebra. The quantity supplied will equal quantity demanded at equilibrium, and the supply price will equal the demand price. Let $575 + 8Q = 920 - 15Q$, then $345 = 23Q$ so $Q = 15$. $P = 575 + (8 \times 15) = 695$.

347. (A) Let $1,000 + 3Q = 5,000 - 5Q$. Then $8Q = 4,000$ so $Q = 50$. $P = 1,000 + (3 \times 50) = 1,150$.

348. (A) Choice (A) is correct. If the supply curve for apples shifted to the right and the demand curve for apples shifted to the left, the equilibrium price for apples would decrease.

349. (D) Choice (D) is correct. If the supply curve for pears shifted to the right and the demand curve for pears shifted to the right as well, the equilibrium quantity of pears would increase.

350. (A) Choice (A) is correct. If an effective price floor was established for grapes, quantity supplied would be more than quantity demanded.

Chapter 3

351. (D) Choice (D) is the best answer. MFC < MRP so the auto manufacturer should increase output. MFC for machinery is less than MFC for another employee, so the auto manufacturer should buy machinery until marginal output is the same.

352. (A) Derived demand refers to the demand for resources that come from the demand for the goods produced by the resources. Choice (A) is the best answer because the demand for workers comes from the demand for automobiles for consumers to drive.

353. (C) Choice (C) is the best answer. Either buying an oven or hiring five more workers would increase profit by $100 so the taco stand is indifferent between the two choices.

354. (E) Choice (E) is the best answer. Hiring a second employee increases cost by $200 and revenue by $200. Buying one oven increases cost by $400 and revenue by $400. In both cases, MRP = MRC. If the pretzel stand hires a third employee or a second oven, MRP < MRC.

355. (B) Choice (B) is correct. The marginal revenue product of labor (MRP) refers to the change in a firm's total revenue from hiring one additional unit of labor. The best way to calculate the MRP is to multiply the marginal product (producing one more unit of output) by the product price.

356. (D) Choice (D) is the best answer.

357. (A) Choice (A) is the best answer. The other choices would be caused by an increase in demand for popcorn.

358. (D) Choice (D) is the best answer. Manufacturers will minimize costs by hiring workers where the MFC of labor is the lowest.

359. (B) Choice (B) is the best answer. Job training increases worker productivity, which increases the MRP for labor.

360. (E) Choice (E) is correct. The rancher pays $9 for the eleventh bag of feed, plus an additional $1 for each of the first 10 bags, so MFC is $19.

361. (D) Choice (D) is the best answer. Consumers don't demand raw materials, a manufacturer demands raw materials so it can make finished goods for consumers.

362. (A) Choice (A) is correct. A shift from D2 to D3 for bread demand is an increase in demand, increasing demand for wheat because it is an input for bread.

363. (A) Choice (A) is correct. Demand for wheat is a derived demand and demand for wheat is a direct demand because wheat is an input for bread.

364. (D) Choice (D) is correct. The supply of labor would increase and the curve would shift to the right.

365. (C) Choice (C) is correct. Remember the determinants of supply. If there is a new development in technology, it would potentially decrease a firm's cost of production and shift the curve to the right.

366. (A) Choice (A) is the best answer. MRP is $600, $400, and $200 for the first, second, and third worker, respectively. If the MFC for labor was $400, the factory would have two workers. If the MFC for labor was $200, the factory would hire a third worker.

367. (B) Choice (B) is correct. Revenue for four workers is $4 × $100, or $400. Revenue for five workers is $3 × 150, or $450. So MRP for the fifth worker is $50 and MRP = MFC at $50.

368. (C) Choice (C) is correct. Revenue would increase from $2 × 100, or $200, to $1.50 × 200, or $300. Thus, MRP is $100.

369. (C) Choice (C) is the best answer. Because the college canceled its nursing classes, fewer trained nurses will be available for the hospitals to hire.

370. (C) Choice (C) is correct. A higher onion cost would increase the cost of production and the food processor's labor demand curve would shift to the left.

371. (B) Choice (B) is the best answer. If the motorcycle factory can substitute machinery for labor, then it needs fewer workers if machinery becomes more efficient.

372. (D) Choice (D) is the best answer. If machinery and labor are complementary resources, more efficient machines will increase the MRP of labor so the airplane factory will hire more workers.

373. (A) Choice (A) is correct. When demand for a product is elastic, the firm's demand for inputs used to produce the product will be elastic as well.

374. (A) Choice (A) is correct. If substitute inputs are available in the market, the firm's demand for inputs will be more elastic.

375. (A) Choice (A) is the best answer. When a production input is less important, the firm's demand for the input will be more elastic.

376. (B) Choice (B) is the best answer. Company B's MP of labor declines more rapidly because it doesn't have unused trucks available, so company B has more elastic labor demand.

377. (B) Choice (B) is correct. The price elasticity of labor demand is –15 percent/45 percent, which is –0.33.

378. (A) Choice (A) is correct. The price elasticity of labor supply is 20 percent/40 percent, which is 0.5.

379. (A) Choice (A) is correct. If the MFC of labor decreases, employment increases because firms will demand more labor.

380. (A) Choice (A) is correct. Demand for production inputs is a derived demand because consumers don't purchase production inputs themselves.

381. (B) Choice (B) is correct. Consumers demand hamburgers so this is an example of direct demand.

382. (A) Choice (A) is correct. The truck manufacturer hires production workers because consumers demand trucks.

383. (A) Choice (A) is the best answer. The factory will cut back on sugar purchases until MFC = MRP.

384. (B) The correct choice is (B). Adding the ninth employee allows the suit manufacturer to produce (24 – 20) = 4 more suits, which are worth $100 each, so marginal revenue product is $400.

385. (C) Choice (C) is correct. Adding the sixth employee increases output by two refrigerators, which are worth $500 each, so marginal revenue product is $1,000.

386. (D) Choice (D) is correct. Marginal product is –5, so marginal revenue product is $-5 \times \$10$, or –$50.

387. (B) Choice (B) is the best answer. The firm must compare marginal revenue product to marginal factor cost. Even if marginal revenue product increases, if MFC is greater than MRP the firm will earn less profit if it increases output. MFC is less than MRP in this example so the golf club factory should increase production.

388. (A) Choice (A) is correct. MRP is $125 and MR is $2.50, so MP must be 50.

389. (C) Choice (C) is the best answer. Because of derived demand, demand for wood will increase and the price of wood will rise.

390. (A) Choice (A) is correct. Human capital refers to the skills a worker applies on the job. Acquiring human capital increases a worker's value in the marketplace. Human capital is a major factor of production, and any increase in human capital through educational training would increase the productivity of labor.

391. (A) Choice (A) is the best choice because the marginal revenue product (MRP) refers to the change in a firm's total revenue from hiring one additional unit of labor. The demand curve slopes downward because of the law of demand, and the MRP curve slopes downward because as marginal product falls, so does the marginal revenue product. Choices (C), (D), and (E) are incorrect because they would all result in an increase in demand.

392. (C) Choice (C) is correct. Wages are a type of marginal resource cost because they increase as output rises.

393. (C) Choice (C) is correct. Choice (B) is marginal revenue product.

394. (B) Choice (B) is the best answer because of derived demand.

395. (C) Choice (C) is the best answer because tomatoes are an input for ketchup.

396. (C) Choice (C) is the best answer. These items are determinants of labor demand.

397. (D) Choice (D) is correct. MRP now equals MFC at $150, instead of $130, so the hot dog truck will lay off its third and fourth workers.

398. (B) Choice (B) is correct. Labor costs would increase by ($5,000 × 7) + $30,000, or $65,000.

399. (A) Choice (A) is correct. The price of a factor of production increased, so the price of another unit of output increases as well.

400. (B) Choice (B) is correct. A monopsony will not employ as many workers as a market with pure competition.

401. (A) Choice (A) is the best answer, because MFC < MRP and the MFC for another employee is less than the MFC for machinery.

402. (B) Choice (B) is the best answer because a monopsony in a factor market is where a sole firm has total market power.

403. (C) Choice (C) is the best answer because wheat is a factor of production for producing bagels. If the price of a factor of production decreases, Seth can increase production and his demand for labor will increase.

404. (B) Choice (B) is the correct answer because derived demand refers to the demand for resources that come from the demand for the goods produced by the resources. Choice (A) is incorrect because it refers to the demand for labor. Choice (C) is incorrect because it illustrates the least-cost rule. Choice (D) is incorrect because that is the profit-maximizing point for resource employment. Choice (E) is incorrect because it refers to a monopsony.

405. (C) Choice (C) is correct. Wages are part of MFC so manufacturers will hire workers where MFC is lower and lay off workers where MFC is higher.

406. (B) Choice (B) is the best answer. MRP for labor will increase in New York because of the free education, while it will fall in Nebraska because fewer students can afford university education.

407. (A) Derived demand refers to the demand for resources that come from the demand for the goods produced by the resource. People have a demand not for the worker but for the product the worker produces. Choice (A) is the best answer because the demand for tractors and workers is derived from people's demand for food.

408. (C) Choice (C) is the best answer because many people go to the doctor when they catch a cold. If a cure is found for the common cold, people will have fewer doctor visits and would decrease the demand for doctors in the long run. Every other choice would increase the demand for doctors.

409. (A) Choice (A) is correct. The output effect states that there will be a rise in output if the price of a resource used in the production of a product decreases, and firms will increase production and the demand for labor will increase.

410. (B) Choice (B) is correct. Remember that the MRP curve and the labor demand curve are similar in that they are both downward sloping. If MRP increases, so will labor demand.

411. (B) Choice (B) is correct. Choice (A) is incorrect because it refers to the marginal revenue cost. Choice (C) is incorrect because it refers to the least-cost rule. Choice (D) is incorrect because it refers to profit maximizing. Choice (E) is incorrect because it refers to a monopsony. The marginal revenue product of labor (MRP) refers to the change in a firm's total revenue from hiring one additional unit of labor.

412. (D) Choice (D) is correct. The firm should lay off workers until MRP of labor equals the wage of the last worker hired.

413. (C) Choice (C) is correct. Immigration will affect a labor supply curve because if it decreases, it will shift that country's labor supply curve to the left. The labor supply curve will shift to the right for the country the labor supply enters.

414. (C) Choice (C) is correct. If the price of raw materials increases, MFC will increase. The firm will have to lay off workers until MRP equals the MFC of labor again.

415. (A) Choice (A) is correct. Remember that complements are products that are used with another product. For example, you cannot play tennis without a racket and tennis balls. If the price of a good increases, so will the price of its complements. This will result in a decrease in labor because firms will lay off workers until MRP = W.

416. (C) Choice (C) is the best answer because the least-cost rule seeks to find the best combination between resources and capital that would be the cheapest for the firm. Choice (A) is incorrect because it refers to a monopsony and the answer does not fully answer the question. Choice (B) is incorrect because it refers to profit maximizing. Choice (D) is incorrect because it refers to marginal revenue cost. Choice (E) is incorrect because it refers to the marginal revenue product.

417. (A) Choice (A) is correct. Equilibrium occurs when MRP = MFC.

418. (A) Choice (A) is the best answer because consumers do not demand the workers themselves; rather, they demand the products the workers produce. Therefore, labor is a derived demand.

419. (B) Choice (B) is correct. Wages are a major cost to firms. If the price of labor increases, then firms will lay off workers to the point where MRP = MFC.

420. (B) Choice (B) is the best answer. Because diners want to eat food at the restaurant (demand), the restaurant will demand cooking ingredients (inputs used to make food).

421. (D) The correct choice is (D). With one more unit of input (the sixth worker) production increases by five auto parts, so MP = 5. The auto parts are worth $3, so MR is $3. MR × MP is $3 × 5, or $15.

422. (D) Choice (D) is correct. For the tenth employee, production increases by three ice cream cones (27 − 24 = 3) so MP = 3. The ice cream cones sell for $2, so MR is $2. MR × MP is $2 × 3, or $6.

423. (D) Choice (D) is correct. If the fishing boat hires a seventh crew member, it brings back five fewer fish. As a result, MP = −5 for the seventh crew member. MR is $4 so MR × MP is $4 × −5, or −$20. The boat has limited space available, so if it hires too many crew members they will get in each other's way and productivity will drop.

424. (D) Choice (D) is the best answer. If the hot dog stand hired a fifth worker, marginal factor cost would increase by $120, while marginal revenue product would increase by 20 × $5 = $100. Thus, MFC is greater than MRP and the hot dog stand shouldn't hire the fifth worker.

425. (A) Choice (A) is the best answer. If graphite is used to make golf clubs and demand for golf clubs increases, golf club manufacturers will demand more graphite and the demand curve for graphite will shift to the right. As a result, the price of graphite will increase.

426. (D) Choice (D) is correct. MRP is $150 and MR is $3, so MP must be 50.

427. (B) Choice (B) is correct. The surfboard manufacturer's decision to hire a seventh worker increases total revenue by $100, so MRP is $100. MP increased by 2, so MR is $100 divided by 2, or $50.

428. (A) Choice (A) is the best answer. In a market with perfect competition, the market price will stay the same if a firm increases output. If a firm has a monopoly, increasing output will cause the market price to fall so MR will decrease as output increases.

429. (C) Choice (C) is the best answer. Again, if perfect competition exists, labor and raw materials costs will remain constant as output increases because firms aren't large enough for their production decisions to affect supply. If the market is a monopsony or an oligopsony, a firm will incur higher labor and raw materials costs if it increases output.

430. (C) Choice (C) is the best answer. All of the other choices would result in higher demand for cars.

431. (A) Choice (A) is correct. The demand for corn increased because corn is an input for corn tortillas and demand for corn tortillas increased.

432. (C) Choice (C) is correct. MFC = $120 and the hot dog stand should hire workers until MRP = MFC.

433. (B) Choice (B) is correct. MFC increased so the equilibrium point where MRP = MFC has moved from $85 to $90.

434. (C) Choice (C) is correct. The skateboard manufacturer is a monopsony. If the firm hired another worker, it would have to pay $50,000 plus $10,000 × 10 in additional labor costs. Thus, MFC is $150,000 and MRP is $60,000, so hiring another employee would reduce profit.

435. (D) Choice (D) is correct. Adding another employee increases labor costs by $40,000 + ($10,000 × 6), or $100,000, so MFC is $100,000.

436. (E) Choice (E) is correct. The firm pays $250 plus (10 × $50) to buy another ton of sugar, so MFC is $750.

437. (A) Choice (A) is correct. If the price of a factor of production decreases, the marginal cost of another unit of output decreases as well.

438. (A) Choice (A) is correct. An oligopsony will have lower wages because firms will not hire as many workers as they would with perfect competition.

439. (C) Choice (C) is correct. Consumers don't demand aluminum, they demand bicycles, so the bicycle manufacturer buys aluminum to satisfy bicycle demand.

440. (A) Choice (A) is correct. Frosting demand will shift to the right because of derived demand, increasing the frosting price and quantity.

Chapter 4

441. (C) Choice (C) is the best answer because the spillover effect refers to additional benefits to society from the production of a good. Chris's neighbors all benefit from Chris's work without incurring any of the costs.

442. (E) Choice (E) is correct. If a good is produced that not all people enjoy the benefit of, it is known as a private good. A private good is a good that can rival other goods and is excludable to other consumers. For example, if a person does not have the money to pay for a taxi, then he or she is forced to find another mode of transportation.

443. (A) Choice (A) is correct. If a positive externality is produced, a person who does not consume or work on the product benefits from it nonetheless. This is known as a marginal external benefit (MEB). The demand curve would not reflect MEB, unless the government intervened and internalized it.

444. (C) Choice (C) is correct. Taxes such as a progressive tax help with the redistribution of wealth.

445. (B) A negative externality refers to costs in the production of goods and services that are put upon a third party. For example, pollution is an example of a negative externality. Therefore, any answer that describes a benefit to society should be eliminated. Choice (B) is the best answer. Choice (A) is incorrect because it describes egalitarianism.

446. (C) Choice (C) is correct. A free rider is a person who benefits from goods and services without incurring any of the costs. The goal of a private firm is to earn a profit, and if free riders are enjoying the benefits of a good or service, then firms do not produce.

447. (C) Choice (C) is correct. A positive externality refers to the benefits experienced by a third party outside the production of a good or service. Therefore, any choice that describes a cost to society should be eliminated. Choice (A) is incorrect because it describes egalitarianism.

448. (A) Choice (A) is correct. If society would benefit when the good has a higher price and a lower quantity produced, then a negative externality exists.

449. (E) Choice (A) is correct. Some of the powers of the government to help the economy grow and be competitive are regulation and antitrust laws. In a completely free market, there is a risk of firms creating monopolies on the market. The government ensures competition (which ensures reasonable prices for goods and services) through regulation and antitrust laws.

450. (A) The graph represents a shift of the demand curve to the right. Eliminate any answer that would lessen or weaken consumers' purchasing power. Choice (A) is the best choice because a government subsidy decreases the impact on people's wallets. This would shift the demand curve to the right.

451. (D) Choice (D) is correct. If a positive externality is produced, a person who does not consume or work on the product benefits from it nonetheless. This is known as a marginal external benefit (MEB). The demand curve would not reflect MEB, unless the government intervened and internalized it.

452. (A) Through regulation, the government may impose restrictions on producers, such as a tax. The graph illustrates a leftward shift of the supply curve. Therefore, eliminate any answer that incorporates a rightward shift of the supply curve. Choice (A) is the best answer.

453. (B) Choice (B) is correct because since the government intervened and shifted the supply curve to the left, production will decrease and the negative externality of overproduction will be corrected.

454. (D) Choice (D) is correct. A free rider is a person who benefits from goods and services without incurring any of the costs. The goal of a private firm is to earn a profit, and if free riders are enjoying the benefits of a good or service, then firms do not produce.

455. (D) Choice (D) is correct. An ability to pay tax is also known as a progressive tax: tax rates should vary according to one's ability to pay them. If a person or company earns a higher income, then that person or company should pay more taxes than those who make less.

456. (A) Choice (A) is correct. A tax is regressive if the proportion of income paid in taxes decreases as income increases. A sales tax is an example of this because people with low incomes pay a higher portion of their money on sales tax compared to people with high incomes.

457. (A) Choice (A) is correct. Compensating differential refers to the measurement between the unpleasantness of a job and wage. For example, a firefighter is doing a more dangerous job than a telemarketer. It does not place the value of one job over the other; it only says that these jobs are different. Although college professors may be more esteemed in the workforce due to their level of education, many plumbers earn more money. The key difference is the nonmonetary differences of a job.

458. (D) Choice (D) is the best answer because the fighter jet is purchased by the government, not an individual consumer, and all domestic consumers receive its national defense benefits.

459. (C) Choice (C) is correct. A proportional tax is a tax that is paid from someone's income regardless of income level and is also known as a "flat tax."

460. (D) Since a negative externality in the form of pollution emerged, a government intervention would focus on the producers of the pollution. Any choice that refers to a government intervention on the part of consumers may be eliminated. Choice (C) is incorrect because it would decrease costs for producers and may lead to an increase in production. Choice (D) is the best answer because a per-unit tax on producers would increase costs and result in a decrease in production and hopefully pollution.

461. (C) Choice (C) is correct. A proportional tax is a tax where the same proportion of income is paid in taxes regardless of income level. Anna received a raise in salary, but she still paid 20 percent of her income in taxes.

462. (D) A public good is a good that is nonexcludable. Choice (D) is the best choice because firefighters must respond to help, regardless if the person paid his or her taxes.

463. (A) A Gini ratio is a measure of income inequality. If the Gini ratio is closer to zero, income distribution is more equal. If the Gini ratio is closer to 1, income distribution is more unequal. Choice (A) is the best answer because this illustrates the definition of a Gini ratio.

464. (E) Choice (E) is correct. The diagram is called a Lorenz curve: a graph that illustrates how a nation's income is distributed throughout a nation's households.

465. (A) Choice (A) is the best answer because a Gini ratio of 0.9 is very close to 1; therefore, it shows a highly unequal distribution of income.

466. (E) Choice (E) is the best answer because this scenario represents a regressive tax. A regressive tax is a tax where the proportion of income paid in taxes decreases as income rises. There is a big difference in salaries between Anna and Sarah, yet Sarah pays only $2,000 more in taxes than Anna.

467. (A) Choice (A) is the best answer because a free market system, without any aid in government intervention, often results in unequal distribution of wealth.

468. (A) Choice (A) is correct. A regressive tax is a tax where the proportion of income paid in taxes decreases as income rises. Choice (B) is incorrect because a proportional tax is a tax that is paid from someone's income regardless of income level. Choice (C) is incorrect because a flat tax is the same as a proportional tax. Choice (D) is incorrect because a progressive tax is a tax where the proportion of income paid in taxes increases as income increases. Choice (E) is incorrect because a tax bracket is based on a person's income level: as your income increases, you might fall into a tax bracket that pays higher taxes.

469. (A) Choice (A) is correct. A progressive tax is a tax where the proportion of income paid in taxes increases as income increases.

470. (B) Choice (B) is correct. A private good is a good that can rival other goods and is excludable to other consumers. If a person does not have the money to pay for a taxicab ride, then he or she is forced to find another mode of transportation.

471. (D) Choice (D) is correct. Since the world benefited from this satellite transmission, the satellite is a public good. A public good is a good that is nonexcludable.

472. (C) Choice (C) is the best answer because taxes like a progressive tax help with the redistribution of wealth. Choice (A) is incorrect because other economic systems help in the redistribution of wealth, such as a mixed economic system. Choice (D) is incorrect because it does not differentiate income levels on the percentage of tax paid.

473. (C) Choice (C) is correct. A Pigovian tax increases the market price of a good to the point where it equals the marginal social cost of the good.

474. (D) Choice (D) is correct. A Pigovian subsidy reduces the market price of a good to the point where the marginal social benefit of the good equals supply.

475. (D) Choice (D) is correct. Vice taxes are applied to goods with negative externalities to limit their consumption, so they are an example of a Pigovian tax.

476. (C) Choice (C) is the best answer. A Pigovian subsidy increases consumption of a product with positive externalities, such as electric vehicles.

477. (D) Choice (D) is correct. The shopkeeper's income rose and the total tax remained the same, so the pension tax is a regressive tax.

478. (B) Choice (B) is the best answer. The marginal cost of air pollution to society is $10 per barrel, so charging gas stations a tax of $10 per barrel would make the marginal social cost of fuel equal the marginal social benefit of fuel.

479. (A) Choice (A) is the best answer. A Pigovian subsidy paid to bus companies will increase the supply of buses, shifting the bus supply curve to the right.

480. (A) Choice (A) is the best answer. A Pigovian subsidy paid to consumers will shift demand for the subsidized good to the right.

481. (B) Choice (B) is the best answer. A police car provides law enforcement for all citizens without charging additional fees and the service is non-rival because police normally have enough cars to enforce the law for all citizens.

482. (A) Choice (A) is the best answer. The Gini ratio fell, so the income distribution in country X became more equal.

483. (B) Choice (B) is the best answer. The Gini ratio increased, so the income distribution in country Y became less equal.

484. (D) Choice (D) is correct. Country B has a lower Gini ratio than country C so it has a more equal income distribution.

485. (B) Choice (B) is correct. The progressive tax will result in a more equal income distribution, and a lower Gini ratio, for country E.

486. (B) Choice (B) is correct. The regressive tax will result in a less equal income distribution, and a higher Gini ratio, for city C.

487. (B) Choice (B) is the best answer. While the birds are a nonexcludable resource, there is a limited supply of birds, so they are a rival good as well. Thus, they are a common resource and not a public good.

488. (C) Choice (C) is the best answer. If the bridge has sufficient capacity, it is a nonrival good. The bridge does have a toll, so it is an excludable resource. Thus, the bridge is a quasi-public good.

489. (D) Choice (D) is correct. When there is little traffic, the freeway is a public good because it is nonexcludable and non-rival. During rush hour, the freeway becomes a rival good (while remaining nonexcludable) so it becomes a common resource. High utilization can also change a quasi-public good into a private good temporarily.

490. (A) Choice (A) is the best answer. Consumers can reach an agreement on negative externalities without government intervention when negotiating costs are low. Reaching an agreement requires MC = MB.

491. (A) Choice (A) is the best answer. The pollution affects many people in the city, which complicates the negotiation process and makes the factory's liabilities unclear. It would be more effective for government regulators to set a price on the pollution caused by the factory.

492. (B) Choice (B) is correct. If society would benefit if production increased and the price fell, a positive externality exists.

493. (E) Choice (E) is the best answer. Subsidized student loans are a consumer subsidy. If grants are available to all students, university education is nonexcludable (since anyone can get a grant) and rival (since universities can admit a limited number of students) so it is also a common resource.

494. (D) Choice (D) is the best answer. A property tax exemption would benefit universities directly, subsidizing the producer. If many students still can't afford tuition, university education is excludable, as well as rival because universities can admit a limited number of students.

495. (B) Choice (B) is the best answer. The government used resources to educate its citizens, and businesses received the spillover benefit of a more productive workforce. Choice (E) is not correct because an alternative to publicly funded education is firms providing education and charging tuition fees.

496. (D) Choice (D) is the best answer. Demand for public goods is considered a phantom demand. An individual does not decide to purchase one unit of a public good by considering the marginal benefits and costs of buying one more unit.

497. (B) Choice (B) is the best answer. The demand curve for a public good is the vertical sum of each consumer's demand curve.

498. (D) Choice (D) is correct. This graph shows demand curves for a public good.

499. (D) Choice (D) is correct. The vertical sum of MB1, MB2, and MB3 (MB SUM) = MC at the equilibrium price of the public good.

500. (B) Choice (B) is correct. For a public good, the sum of consumers' demand curves will decline more sharply than the demand curve for an individual consumer.